AMERICAN HERITAGE
ILLUSTRATED HISTORY
OF THE UNITED STATES

Infantrymen go down the cargo net and into a boat for the Normandy landing in 1944.
U.S. COAST GUARD

FRONT COVER: *The Japanese strike Pearl Harbor in this detail of a U.S. Navy artist's painting of the December 7, 1941 attack.*
U.S. NAVY: COMBAT ART SECTION

FRONT ENDSHEET: *On December 7, 1941, the "date that will live in infamy," the Japanese launch a surprise attack on the U.S. fleet at Pearl Harbor, sinking eight battleships and three cruisers.*
U.S. NAVY ART SECTION

CONTENTS PAGE: *A wartime poster urges Allied unity in the face of the enemy.*
WEST POINT MUSEUM

BACK ENDSHEET: *General MacArthur looks on as General Yoshijiro Umezu signs the Japanese surrender document aboard the U.S.S. Missouri in Tokyo Bay on September 2, 1945.*
DEPARTMENT OF THE NAVY

BACK COVER: *General Dwight D. Eisenhower (top left), the Supreme Commander of the Allied troops, addresses paratroopers as they prepare for the D-Day invasion; A wartime poster (top right) dramatizes the contribution of women who went to work in factories to keep the supply lines filled; Churchill, Roosevelt, and Stalin (bottom) meet at Yalta in 1945 to discuss the postwar world.*
IMPERIAL WAR MUSEUM, LONDON; FRANKLIN D. ROOSEVELT LIBRARY; FRANKLIN D. ROOSEVELT LIBRARY

AMERICAN HERITAGE
ILLUSTRATED HISTORY
OF THE UNITED STATES

VOLUME 15

WORLD WAR II

BY ROBERT G. ATHEARN

Created in Association with the
Editors of AMERICAN HERITAGE

and for the updated edition
MEDIA PROJECTS INCORPORATED

CHOICE PUBLISHING, INC.
New York

Library of Congress Catalog Number: 87-7399
ISBN 0-945260-15-6

This 1988 edition is published and distributed by Choice Publishing, Inc., 53 Watermill Lane, Great Neck, NY 11021
by arrangement with American Heritage, a division of Forbes, Inc.

Manufactured in the United States of America

CONTENTS OF THE COMPLETE SERIES

Editor's Note to the Revised Edition
Introduction by ALLAN NEVINS
Main text by ROBERT G. ATHEARN

EACH VOLUME CONTAINS AN ENCYCLOPEDIC SECTION; MASTER INDEX IN VOLUME 18

CONTENTS OF VOLUME 15

CHAPTER 43

BACKGROUND FOR WAR

Americans were so engrossed in a major battle for economic survival during the 1930s that many of them found it hard to realize that Europe, once so remote, so safely distant, was now coming dangerously near.

The principal cause for alarm was the power politics of dictators Adolf Hitler and Benito Mussolini and the Japanese military. Mussolini had come to power in Italy in 1922, and for a time, many Americans were disposed to regard him well, as a man who brought order, who "made the trains run on time." Then, in 1935, he picked a quarrel with Ethiopia, a primitive kingdom whose armed forces used spears and muzzle-loading rifles, and the world waited to see what the League of Nations would do about the aggression. Although the United States invoked an arms embargo and the league imposed economic sanctions, Italy was not to be put off. France in particular was afraid that the pressure would drive Mussolini

As the United States went to war again for the second time in 24 years, Norman Rockwell did this painting of the American soldier from the time of the Revolution.

closer to Hitler. In a six-month campaign, Italy completed its conquest.

Japanese generals and admirals who had been making and breaking governments in their homeland since 1900 attacked and occupied Manchuria in 1931 and followed up the gain with a drive into China in 1933. The United States, struggling through the worst of the depression, stood by and did nothing despite the protests of Secretary of State Henry L. Stimson.

In Germany, Adolf Hitler, an Austrian who had been a corporal in the German army in World War I, had been attempting to seize power with his National Socialist Party since 1923. By 1933, a combination of Hitler's great oratorical ability, wide unemployment, and the business community's fear of the German Communist Party enabled him to emerge as chancellor and soon thereafter as legal dictator. When war-hero President Paul von Hindenburg died in 1934, Hitler became *der Führer* (the leader) and quickly rearmed Germany despite the Treaty of Versailles.

To many Americans, Italy's adventure in Ethiopia and Japan's in China seemed far away, but the boldness of

British Prime Minister Neville Chamberlain thought he had made "peace in our time" by giving Hitler the Sudetenland.

Hitler's moves was of much greater concern. His policy of violent anti-Semitism was cause for alarm throughout the Jewish community in the United States. His effective assistance to rebel General Francisco Franco in the Spanish Civil War, beginning in 1936, was proof of his growing power. In the same year, he remilitarized the Rhineland, against the advice of his own generals. France and Britain did nothing. Screaming that the German people wanted "guns instead of butter," he annexed Austria in 1938, chipped the Sudetenland off Czechoslovakia, and then took over the whole of that unhappy country in March, 1939. In September, 1938, Britain's Prime Minister Neville Chamberlain had gone to Munich, acquiesced in the Czechoslovakian seizure, and returned to London to announce, "I believe it is peace in our time."

Russia's Foreign Minister Maxim Litvinov worked hard for an alliance between his own country, Britain, and France against Hitler, but the French and English could not bring themselves to become partners with the Communists. Then, Russian dictator Joseph Stalin made his own non-aggression treaty with Hitler. Coming up with too little too late, Chamberlain made a unilateral guarantee to protect Poland, Hitler's next target. Hitler calculated that he could defeat Poland before England could act, and on September 1, 1939, struck with tanks, infantry, and Stuka dive bombers. Russia promptly attacked from the east, and before the month was out, a brave Polish army, which contained such anachronisms as lancer cavalry, collapsed. As Hitler had foreseen, the British and French declared war, but did little but sit behind France's supposedly impregnable Maginot Line.

America views the war

Official American reaction to the outbreak of hostilities in Europe was similar to that of 1914: The President proclaimed neutrality. On September 3, 1939, he said, "I hope the United States will keep out of this war. I believe that it will. And I give you assurances that every effort of your government will be directed toward that end." However, unlike Woodrow Wilson, Franklin D. Roosevelt did not ask the people to be neutral in thought as well as deed. He admitted that "even a neutral has a right to take account of the facts." By this attitude, he acknowledged that the situation was somewhat different from that of 1914. This time, American public opinion was heavily in favor of the Allies.

In Roosevelt's neutrality proclamation of September 5, he had declared an embargo on the shipment of arms to belligerents. Later that month, he called Congress into special session and asked for a revision of the existing neutrality laws. Congress responded by lifting the arms embargo, but it retained the prohibition of loans to belligerents. By this action, it attempted to do two things—first, to maintain America's traditional policy of shipping goods to any and all and, second, to stay free of involvement with one side similar to that of 1914–17 which, some people felt, developed from the policy of making loans to England. The act, passed on November 4, also barred United States ships from war zones and forbade American citizens to travel on the ships of belligerent nations. Memories of the Americans who died when the Germans torpedoed the British liner *Lusitania* in 1915 still haunted the legislators.

Nevertheless, an effort was made to help the Allies without entering into

Adolf Hitler was boss of the Rome-Berlin axis. His partner, Benito Mussolini, was sometimes called the Sawdust Caesar.

any military participation. The United States was willing to sell them goods provided it did not have to deliver them. This "cash and carry" policy put a tremendous strain on the British merchant marine, which, under effective attack from German submarines, lost approximately 3,000,000 tons of shipping during the first year of the war.

The Neutrality Act was the high point of American determination to stay out of the war. From that time on, the administration moved gradually toward the conviction that the conflict was a struggle to save democratic civilization and that the United States had a share of responsibility in it. Even in 1939, a good many Americans did not object to all-out aid short of war. A Gallup poll taken that fall showed that 62% of the people were in favor of helping the Allies by sending materials, while 84% picked them as likely winners. Only 2% favored the Germans, while 14% had no opinion. At that time, 5% of those polled favored an immediate declaration of war on Germany, and 29% were willing to take that course if Germany appeared to be winning.

American preparedness

Although Roosevelt, Assistant Secretary of the Navy in World War I, had been building up the fleet since the mid-'30s, further enlargement of all the armed forces was necessary, and to do it effectively would require a draft. This would not only be unpopular, it would also be unprecedented, for never in American history had there been peacetime conscription. Early in 1940, Senator Edward R. Burke (Democrat, Nebraska) and Representative James W. Wadsworth (Republican, New York) presented the bill to Congress. The bipartisan nature of the move was underscored when Wendell L. Willkie, Republican Presidential candidate, approved it in his speech accepting the nomination. The Selective Training and Service Act, approved September 16, 1940, called for the registration of all males between the ages of 21 and 35. Those "selected" were to serve for one year—in the Western Hemisphere only. On registration day,

October 16, 16,400,000 young men signed up with a minimum of protest. Tin Pan Alley quickly produced *Don't Worry, Dear, I'll Be Back In a Year*. By the time the year was almost over, it was rumored that the increasing gravity of the international situation might mean that many who were in the service would be kept on longer. In the training camps, latrines blossomed with the letters O.H.I.O., for "Over The Hill In October." But October passed and few servicemen went "over the hill" as deserters.

The fleet got a boost in July, 1940, with the passage of a billion-dollar appropriation designed to build a two-ocean navy and increase total tonnage by 70%. It also provided for a 15,000-plane naval air arm.

In May and June, the German *blitzkrieg*, or "lightning war," had swept through Belgium, Holland, and France. Those countries were occupied, and a badly battered British Expeditionary Force barely got home from the beaches around the French port of Dunkirk. During the summer of 1940, the great Battle of Britain was fought. The victory of the Royal Air Force over Hitler's bombers staved off a possible invasion, but it did not assure permanent immunity from Nazi attack.

Roosevelt took another step toward war in the fall of 1940. In exchange for 99-year leases on bases in Newfoundland, Bermuda, the Bahamas, Jamaica, British Guiana, Trinidad, and other smaller locations, he turned

Pinned against the sea at Dunkirk, 233,000 British and some 100,000 French troops were rescued by a pickup fleet of naval, merchant, and civilian craft.

over 50 World War I American destroyers to Great Britain. This was of great assistance militarily, but the British were in severe financial straits. If they were to continue their war effort, supplies from America could not be denied them.

Roosevelt's answer was "Lend-Lease." First, he sought and found a legal basis for what he was about to propose—in a law of 1892 that said the President could, through the Secretary of War, lend army property "not required for the public use" for a period up to five years. Then he went before the people in one of his radio "fireside chats" and explained the problem in a simple parable. "Suppose my neighbor's home catches fire, and I have a length of garden hose," he began. "Now what do I do? I don't say to him, 'Neighbor, my garden hose cost me $15; you have to pay me $15 for it.' What *is* the transaction that goes on? I don't want the $15; I want my garden hose

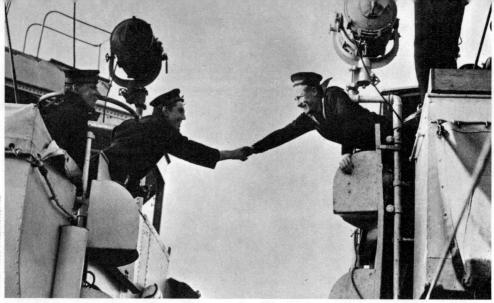

British sailors congratulate each other on arriving safely, after helping bring to England two of the 50 overage American destroyers lend-leased by Roosevelt.

back when the fire is over." Roosevelt then spelled out the parallel: Without American aid, Britain would go down and war would come to the American doorstep. "We must," he concluded, "become the arsenal of democracy."

From the beginning of American aid to the Allies there had been a numerically small but highly vocal opposition. It ranged from the Nazi-like members of the German-American Bund to pacifists—citizens who believed that wars were incited by munitions manufacturers and citizens who simply couldn't understand that the world had changed since George Washington warned against getting entangled in European affairs. From all these groups came an outcry against Lend-Lease. In Congress, Senator Burton K. Wheeler (Democrat, Montana) said it was "the New Deal's Triple-A foreign policy: it will plow under every fourth American boy." (This was a reference to the Agricultural Adjustment Act of 1933, which provided for the curtailment of crop production to reduce surpluses.) Such prominent Americans as Herbert Hoover and Charles A. Lindbergh made speeches against the administration's program. Senator Robert A. Taft (Republican, Ohio), who had nearly won his party's nomination in 1940, went along with lend-leasing to Britain, but opposed giving anything to Russia, which Hitler, in violation of his treaty with Stalin, had invaded in June, 1941. Despite the protests from those who wanted to aid "America first" (and thus became known as America Firsters), the Lend-Lease Bill passed Congress with an initial appropriation of $7,000,000,000 to implement it.

Obviously, Roosevelt intended to go far beyond the law of 1892. America would order huge quantities of new equipment for shipment to Britain. To help solve the problem of getting it overseas, Roosevelt set up a "neutrality patrol," which was in fact nothing but an innocent-sounding name for a system whereby the United States Navy convoyed British shipping to an Atlantic midway point at which British escorts picked it up. To provide additional tonnage, the government seized 28 Italian and two German ships it had impounded early in the war. Thirty-five Danish vessels, caught in American ports when the Nazis overran Denmark, were taken over. The President obtained from the Danish minister in Washington (acting for his imprisoned king) the right to build air bases in Greenland. United States troops occupied Iceland. The bridge to Britain was almost complete.

Through the summer of 1941, the Germans drove deeply into Russia. At the same time in the Atlantic, their submarines, operating in "wolf packs," sent British shipping losses soaring so high that London stopped publishing the figures. Supplying the new ally, Russia, through its northern port of Murmansk was even harder than supplying Britain. Convoys bound there were exposed not only to submarines but also to surface ships and aircraft based in Nazi-occupied Norway. Some Americans distrusted Russia as an ally and agreed with Senator Wheeler when he said, "Just let Joe Stalin and the other dictators fight it out." Roosevelt, however, sent Harry Hopkins to Moscow to evaluate Russian intentions. The special envoy reported that he was convinced the Russians would not make a separate peace with Germany and that they should be strongly supported.

Diplomats at sea

Toward mid-August, 1941, Franklin Roosevelt and British Prime Minister Winston Churchill met off the Newfoundland coast in a historic conference. Aboard the American cruiser *Augusta*, the two men discussed the direction the war had taken and made plans to cooperate more extensively in stopping the Axis powers. Out of

Ohio Senator Robert A. Taft was a leading Republican exponent of isolationism but later voted for the United Nations.

Roosevelt and British Prime Minister Winston Churchill met on a ship at sea and drew up the historic Atlantic Charter, which stated their war aims.

the long conversations came a formalized set of principles that was to become known as the Atlantic Charter. In its eight points, many heard an echo of Wilson's Fourteen Points of 1918. First, it stated that neither the United States nor Great Britain sought aggrandizement. It went on to say that these powers hoped that after the war there would be no territorial changes not in accord with the wishes of the people concerned and that all people would have the right to choose the form of government under which they wished to live. Further, they

looked for the closest cooperation between all nations, victors and vanquished, in the economic field—to the end that world living standards might be raised and that all might live free of fear and want. Finally, "All nations of the world, for realistic as well as spiritual reasons, must come to the abandonment of the use of force."

The first shots

The Germans could hardly be expected to sit by and watch American aid flow to England unimpeded. In May, the American freighter *Robin*

1272

Moor was sunk. Early September saw the United States destroyer *Greer* attacked by a submarine near Iceland, and later that same month, another freighter, the *L. C. White*, went down off Brazil. In mid-October, the destroyer *Kearny* was torpedoed near Iceland but not sunk, and then the U.S.S. *Reuben James,* another destroyer, was sunk in the same neighborhood with a heavy loss of life. Roosevelt said the German policy was one of "international lawlessness" designed to abolish freedom of the seas, but in all fairness, the United States could no longer, even by the most wishful thinking, be called a neutral. On September 11, the President announced that the time had passed when American ships and planes would wait until the Nazi U-boats attacked. Enemy submarines found within the United States defense zone were to be sunk on sight.

In addition, Roosevelt asked for repeal of several parts of the Neutrality Act—the prohibition against arming merchantmen; bans upon entry of American ships into combat zones; and the denial of belligerent ports to American vessels. It took Congress two months to debate the changes, with isolationists strongly opposing them. But the sinking of the *Reuben James* helped bring the issue to a vote. The Senate supported the President, 50 to 37, and the House followed a week later, on November 13,

Japanese Special Envoy Saburo Kurusu, Secretary of State Cordell Hull, and Ambassador Kichisaburo Nomura met and conferred just before Pearl Harbor.

but with a much narrower margin, 212 to 194.

Relations with Japan

American relations with Japan had been deteriorating since the seizure of Manchuria and the China invasion in the early '30s. The United States refused to accept the Japanese position that she had special rights in China, and in 1939, Secretary of State Cordell Hull announced that a 1911 trade treaty with Japan would not be renewed. The following year, a large new loan was made to China and an embargo was put on shipments of scrap iron and steel to Japan. In 1940, after the fall of France, Tokyo decided it was time to get on the Axis band wagon, and their ambassador to Berlin, Saburo Kurusu—who would later keep Cordell Hull talking while the Japanese fleet steamed toward Pearl Harbor—signed a military alliance with Germany and Italy. That year Japan also proclaimed a sort of Monroe Doctrine for Asia, declaring that the Orient should be a single economic sphere under Japanese influence.

In September, 1940, in spite of warnings from American Secretary of State Cordell Hull that further aggression would have most serious effects on American public opinion, the Japanese put pressure on the French, then lying helpless under the Nazi heel, for concessions in Indochina. Japanese troops occupied the country little by little and had it all by June, 1941. Pressure was also put on Holland for Indonesia. Great Britain and the United States promptly froze all Japanese assets and intensified the existing economic blockade.

In Tokyo, General Hideki Tojo became prime minister and the army suppressed all opposition political parties. On November 11, Secretary of the Navy Frank Knox warned that conflict in the Pacific was a distinct possibility. Undersecretary of State Sumner Welles echoed the warning. In November, Japan sent Special Envoy Kurusu—who had signed with the Axis—to Washington to give the United States "a last opportunity to make amends for past aggressions." Secretary Hull complained that the Japanese words were far from peaceful, and he cautioned them not to bluff, for, he said, the United States would not. On Saturday, December 6, President Roosevelt cabled a personal message to Emperor Hirohito asking him to help preserve the peace.

Hull met with Kurusu and Japanese ambassador Kichisaburo Nomura on Sunday, December 7, to hear their response to Roosevelt's plea for peace. At a meeting that began at 2:20 p.m., the secretary was informed that Japan had rejected American overtures. The United States was accused of conspiring with other powers to curb the spread of Japanese influence in the Far East and of keeping alive difficulties between Japan and China. Greatly angered, Hull—a caustic Southerner—scolded his callers and labeled the charges "infamous falsehoods."

D–DAY

It was the late spring of 1944, and the Hitler empire, which once stood at the gates of Moscow and the doorway to Suez, had been shrinking. North Africa had fallen, Sicily was gone, the Italian mainland was conquered to Rome and beyond, and Italy was out of the war. The Russians were driving the Nazis from Red soil and at some points were into Rumania and Poland. In the west, though, the German still stood at the Atlantic Wall (above), waiting for the Anglo-American invasion from England. A debate was raging over the defense: Stop the enemy on the beaches or keep a mobile force inland to stop him after landing. Field Marshal Erwin Rommel said, "An attempt must be made to beat off the enemy landing on the coast and to fight the battle in a more or less strongly fortified coastal strip." Adolf Hitler cast his vote with the field marshal.

ASSAULT: "AWAY ALL BOATS!"

IMPERIAL WAR MUSEUM, LONDON

Supreme Allied Commander General Dwight D. Eisenhower planned to drop his paratroopers (above) behind the German defenses and put his infantry ashore under mass bombing (below) and a naval bombardment. On June 5, the weather turned bad. Ike debated and decided: "How long can you hang this operation on the end of a limb? Give the order."

F.P.G.

H-Hour was 6:30 a.m. on June 6. In the hours before dawn, the warships (above, center) bombarded the beaches and the little landing craft circled before forming into the assault waves. The first men ashore took what shelter they could find behind the iron obstacles (below) that Rommel had built in the shallows to tear the bottoms from the landing craft.

Illustrated London News

D–DAY

LUCK ON THE BRITISH BEACHES

The Germans had expected the landing farther north in the Pas de Calais area, which was closest to England, and Eisenhower had deceived them by bombing the site heavily. The ruse worked, tying down German troops, and on two out of three British beaches the men got ashore against second-rate enemy units. Larger landing craft carrying tanks and artillery rammed onto the beaches to give the infantry the weapons needed against the counterattack.

BAD LUCK ON OMAHA

On the Americans' Omaha Beach (below), the story was bloodily different. Unknown to Allied intelligence, a crack German outfit had been moved onto the bluffs covering the beach for coast-defense exercises. These veterans lay low in the shelling, then emerged to inflict casualties as high as 40% on the first units ashore. Officers lost their men in the confusion and made do with pickups. A lieutenant yelled at the men crouching in the shale, "Are you going to lay there and get killed or get up and do something about it?" General Omar Bradley confessed, "I reluctantly contemplated the diversion of Omaha forces to the British beaches."

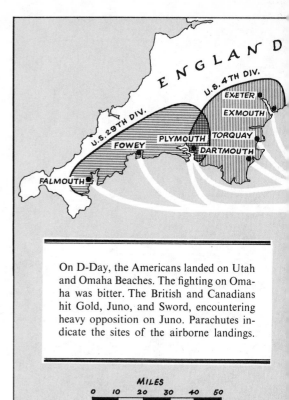

On D-Day, the Americans landed on Utah and Omaha Beaches. The fighting on Omaha was bitter. The British and Canadians hit Gold, Juno, and Sword, encountering heavy opposition on Juno. Parachutes indicate the sites of the airborne landings.

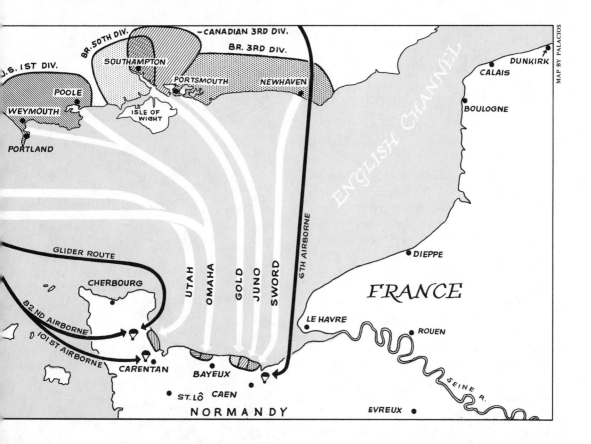

MAP BY PALACIOS

U.S. 1ST DIV.

BR. 50TH DIV.

CANADIAN 3RD DIV.

BR. 3RD DIV.

SOUTHAMPTON

POOLE

WEYMOUTH

PORTSMOUTH

NEWHAVEN

PORTLAND

ISLE OF WIGHT

ENGLISH CHANNEL

DUNKIRK

CALAIS

BOULOGNE

GLIDER ROUTE

CHERBOURG

UTAH OMAHA GOLD JUNO SWORD

6TH AIRBORNE

82 ND AIRBORNE

101 ST AIRBORNE

CARENTAN

BAYEUX

ST. LÔ CAEN

NORMANDY

DIEPPE

FRANCE

LE HAVRE

ROUEN

SEINE R.

EVREUX

COMBAT ART SECTION, U.S. NAVY

FOUL-UP AND SUCCESS ON UTAH

Both the British and American airborne landings were damp. Normandy is cut up with canals and overgrown creeks that Frenchmen call rivers. The British drop near the Orne and Dives Rivers (right) was designed to smash any bridges over which the Germans could bring up support, but to hold one bridge over the Orne by which commandos could come up to help them hold on. It went well. The American drops went badly in the hedgerows behind Utah Beach, but little groups of widely scattered jumpers (below, left) confused the defense. Many of them died in glider crashes or drowned in the marshes (below, right), but by early morning the key town, Ste. Mere-Eglise, had fallen and the Fourth Division driving in over Utah Beach had made it with only 197 casualties and had 20,000 men moving inland.

Illustrated London News

TIME-LIFE COLLECTION, DEPARTMENT OF DEFENSE

STRANGLEHOLD ON THE AIR

IMPERIAL WAR MUSEUM, LONDON

Rommel had advocated the tight defense on the beaches because he had learned during the North African campaign how air power could tie his panzers down. Now he wrote, "Our operations in Normandy are tremendously hampered by the immensely powerful, at times overwhelming, superiority of the enemy air force." Fighter-bombers (left) and rocket-firing fighters (above) closed the roads to his columns during daylight.

D-DAY

"TAKE THE MEN OFF THE BEACH!"

The British (above, left) were ashore and moving on toward Caen. Utah was in good shape, but on Omaha, casualties mounted (left). Acting as if he were bulletproof, American General Norman Cota strode the beach and shouted to "jar the men loose." It was 1:30 p.m. when Omar Bradley got the word "Troops advancing up heights behind the beaches" and German prisoners (above) began coming disconsolately back under guard.

THE DAY ENDS
IN VICTORY

They had done it. By the end of D-Day, a force of 200,000 men had come in over the beaches and three airborne divisions were causing havoc in the enemy rear. The casualties had been lighter than expected—about 10,000 for the job. Men of the First Division (above) pushed on inland, and infantry on ruined German bunkers waved to fighter-bombers (left) flying on to punish the German support. Today a cemetery and a monument (right) stand above Omaha Beach in memory of men who died for a 60-mile-wide part of Fortress Europe.

1289

CHAPTER 44

FROM PEARL HARBOR TO BERLIN AND TOKYO

PAINTING BY TOM LEA, FROM *The Second World War* BY WINSTON CHURCHILL AND THE EDITORS OF *Life.* © 1959 TIME INC.

Even as Ambassador Nomura and Special Envoy Kurusu talked with Hull, the war had begun. A Japanese task force built around six aircraft carriers had been under way since November 26. About 2 p.m. on December 7, reports reached Washington that the carrier-based planes had launched a successful surprise attack on the United States Pacific Fleet at Pearl Harbor, Hawaii. The command at Pearl had been alerted for possible attack on November 27, but had failed to take appropriate action. There was little long-range reconnaissance; aircraft on the ground were not dispersed; vessels anchored along Battleship Row were not put to sea. Only by fortunate accident were the American carriers away on exercises. A radar operator picked up some pips and assumed them to be American bombers expected from the States.

The first wave of Japanese bombers and strafing fighter planes struck at 7:55 a.m., Hawaii time. On one cruiser,

The sea war in the Pacific was chiefly a battle between aircraft carriers. The American flattop Hornet *fights for her life as a Japanese dive bomber crashes into her superstructure (upper right).*

the Catholics in the crew had just left for Mass when the general-quarters—battle-stations—klaxon sounded. On the battleship *Oklahoma,* the public-address system blared, "Real planes, real bombs; this is no drill!" The Japanese pilots had already radioed back to their carriers, "Surprise attack successful." A second wave came over at 8:40 a.m., and when they were through, 18 vessels, including eight battleships and three cruisers, were sunk or severely damaged, 347 aircraft were knocked out—most of them before they could leave the ground—and there were 2,403 Americans dead and 1,178 wounded.

On Monday, Roosevelt went before Congress and announced, "Yesterday, December 7, 1941—a date that will live in infamy—the United States of America was suddenly and deliberately attacked." Congress declared war and repeated the declaration on December 11, when Germany and Italy entered the war against the United States.

Simultaneously with the attack on Pearl Harbor there had been an equally successful attack on American forces based in the Philippines and lesser attacks on Wake and Midway Islands. Japanese land forces drove into Malaya and Thailand.

In spite of the disaster, for the first time in its history when it was not actually at war, the nation was at least partially prepared. Because of the peacetime draft, it had an army of 1,600,000 in various stages of training. When America entered World War I, she had an army of only 92,000. Before World War II was over, more than 15,000,000 men and women would serve in the armed forces.

War on far-flung fronts

One after the other, the Allied outposts in the Pacific fell—Guam, Wake Island, Hong Kong, Malaya, and the Philippines. The fight for the Philippines was bitter, with the forces of General Douglas MacArthur, badly outnumbered, forced to give ground until they were confined to the Bataan Peninsula and finally to the little island of Corregidor—"The Rock"—in Manila Bay. On May 6, 1942, Corregidor surrendered after MacArthur and a few of his staff had been evacuated to Australia by submarine on the order of President Roosevelt. The Japanese moved through the islands of the South Pacific so successfully that worried Americans feared Australia and New Zealand would be taken next.

During these gloomy days, military planners decided on a holding action against the Japanese—to keep them in check while aiming the main blows at Hitler's empire. It was a difficult choice, but Hitler and Mussolini controlled a vast industrial potential in Europe and their threat was, in the long run, greater than that in the East. The danger that Russia might fall before Nazi onslaughts—during the winter of 1941–42, the panzers were at the

In the Battle of the Coral Sea on May 7, 1942, American carrier planes turned back a Japanese force headed for Port Moresby. An American dive bomber pulls out after an attack on the Japanese carrier Shoho.

gates of Moscow—and thus give the enemy a large additional quantity of slave labor and industry deeply concerned the Allies.

Nevertheless, counterblows in the Pacific were quickly struck. By February, 1942, naval task forces built around the carriers that had escaped Pearl Harbor were hitting Japanese-held islands, and on April 18, 16 army medium bombers led by Colonel James H. Doolittle flew off two carriers to strike Tokyo and other Japanese cities. The material damage was minor, but the knowledge that their home islands were vulnerable hurt Japanese and raised American morale.

In May, the Japanese suffered their first real repulse. An American task force located an invasion force aiming for Port Moresby in New Guinea to cut the Australian supply line. The ensuing Battle of the Coral Sea was fought entirely between carrier-based planes—the first naval battle in history in which surface ships did not fire a single shot. The Japanese lost one carrier and had another damaged.

The Americans lost the *Lexington,* and the *Yorktown* was badly damaged. Most important, however, the invasion force was turned back. The Japanese spearhead had been blunted.

Much worse was shortly to come. Fleet Admiral Isoroku Yamamoto was convinced that the United States Pacific Fleet must be destroyed before the end of 1942. After that date, the reinforcements from American war production would make its strength overwhelming. To bring it to battle while the odds were still in his favor, Yamamoto planned to strike at Midway Island, the guardian outpost of Hawaii itself. Admiral Chester W. Nimitz, Commander in Chief of the Pacific Fleet, could not refuse battle. The Japanese had four big carriers and one light carrier against three for the Americans and an overwhelming superiority in battleships and cruisers.

In this seemingly hopeless situation, Admiral Nimitz had two advantages: His staff had succeeded in breaking the Japanese code and knew Yamamoto's plan in detail. One part of it was to send a small Japanese force into the North Pacific as a feint to draw the Americans out of position. Nimitz also had taciturn, grim-faced Raymond A. Spruance, called by Samuel Eliot Morison one of the greatest admirals in American naval history, in command of the carriers *Enterprise* and *Hornet.*

At 6 a.m. on June 4, a Midway patrol plane sighted the Japanese carriers. Admiral Frank Jack Fletcher, the senior officer present, ordered Spruance to head for them and launch his own aircraft as soon as he was within striking range. Fletcher himself would follow in the carrier *Yorktown* as soon as he recovered his search planes. In the meantime, the Japanese had bombed Midway once, but decided it needed another going over. Their planes were on the flight decks being refueled and rearmed when the first of Spruance's groups—the tor-

At Midway—the battle that doomed Japan—planes from three American carriers destroyed four Japanese carriers with the loss of only one American flattop.

Admiral Raymond A. Spruance, shown here during the Battle of Midway, later claimed modestly that all he did was get into action as quickly as possible.

pedo bombers—struck. The Japanese fighter cover and antiaircraft fire was too much for them, however. Only eight planes came out alive, and not a single torpedo found a target.

Torpedo planes come in low, and the Japanese triumph had disastrous final results. Their antiaircraft gunners had been watching the torpedo planes; their fighter cover was down close to the water. Two minutes after the last torpedo strike, American dive bombers arrived at 14,000 feet and were able to attack almost unopposed. First the *Akagi* got it, the bombs and fuel she was feeding her own planes bursting and burning to destroy her. Then *Kaga* took four hits and went down. *Soryu* went next, and only

Hiryu remained to strike back. She succeeded in damaging *Yorktown*, but moments later, an attack from *Enterprise* left *Hiryu* so damaged that she was finished off by her own destroyers. The battle that had begun with four big Japanese carriers against three Americans now stood at no Japanese against two Americans, and the tide of the war in the Pacific had turned for good. The force trying to take Midway limped home beaten.

The defense was now over, and in August came the first counterattack. The First Marine Division landed on Guadalcanal in the Solomon Islands and, aided later by army units, took the islands after a bitter six months' struggle. American battleships and

American sailors operate a 1.1-inch anti-aircraft machine gun in the fierce fighting after the landings on Guadalcanal.

cruisers, still outnumbered by the enemy, had their finest hours of the war as they fought off Japanese surface units convoying reinforcements or coming down to bombard the crucial marine-held airfield.

The tide turns in Africa

Allied efforts to free the European continent began in North Africa, where German and Italian forces were threatening the Suez Canal. During the summer of 1942, Nazi General Erwin Rommel, "The Desert Fox," swept to within 70 miles of Alexandria, and the discouraged Allies were contemplating a retreat into the Middle East. Rommel was at the end of a long supply line, however, and the British navy and air force were effectively interrupting it. In addition, General Bernard L. Montgomery's Eighth Army had been strengthened, mostly with shipments of American tanks. In October, 1942, his mixed force of British, Australians, New Zealanders, Indians, South Africans, and Free French attacked at El Alamein and sent Rommel reeling back toward Tunisia.

On November 8, an American force under General Dwight D. Eisenhower landed in French Morocco and Algeria, and the Axis troops were now pinched into Tunisia from two directions. Rommel was recalled to Germany, and on May 12, 1943, more than 250,000 Germans and Italians laid down their arms and the war in Africa was over.

Meanwhile, Roosevelt and Churchill met with their advisers at Casablanca and decided that the next move would be against Sicily to complete control of the Mediterranean before an attempt was made upon the European mainland.

On July 10, more than 3,200 vessels carried the American Seventh Army under General George S. Patton, Jr., and the British Eighth under Montgomery to Sicily. The American assignment was to secure the western half of the island, and this was done in a three-week campaign. The British were to drive up the east coast and capture Messina—the German escape port to the Italian mainland. The Germans concentrated heavily against Montgomery on ground favorable to the defense, and when the Allies finally entered Messina after more than six weeks' fighting, the Germans had got most of their troops and equipment out.

The fall of Sicily was also the fall of the long-tottering Benito Mussolini. On July 24, the Fascist Grand Council voted him out of office. A new government, under Marshal Pietro Badoglio, was then installed, and it signed an armistice in Sicily on September 3. But the Germans were not caught unprepared. They promptly disarmed the Italians—most of whom were delighted to quit the war in any way they could—and reinstalled Mussolini as a rival to Badoglio. Hitler intended to make the Allies fight for every foot of the mountainous peninsula.

The fight began September 3 when the Eighth Army jumped across the Straits of Messina and started up the Italian boot. Six days later, a British-American army under American General Mark Clark landed at Salerno and found itself in serious trouble. German Field Marshal Albert Kesselring had calculated that Salerno was exactly where the attack would come and had five divisions waiting for it on the rugged hills back of the beaches. For a desperate day, it seemed that the invaders might be thrown back into the sea, but Allied air power and naval gunfire prevailed, and by October 1, Clark's men were in Naples with the Eighth Army abreast of them

During the bitterly contested Salerno landings, a German Messerschmitt 109 fighter-bomber heads down in flames after a near miss on a landing craft.

DEPARTMENT OF THE ARMY

Infantrymen tow a piece of artillery into position during the jungle fighting on New Guinea, where the swamps and disease held up MacArthur's advance.

to the east. Rome was only 120 miles away, but because of the defense put up by Kesselring in the mountains and a bitter, rainy winter that flooded the rivers and turned the front to mud, it would be June, 1944, before the Allies saw the Holy City.

Through Japan's outer defenses

Japan was now on the defensive, but it was a formidable defense, beginning with a string of island bases running from the North Pacific to the Solomons. Behind these lay another string of island outposts, including the bastions of the Philippines and Okinawa. All these had to be penetrated or bypassed before the heart, the Japanese home islands, could be reached.

The outer barrier was to be smashed in a three-stage attack based on a plan to get behind the most strongly defended positions, cut their supply line, and leave them unprovisioned and un-supported. Thus, in the North Pacific, Kiska was bypassed and Attu taken in May, 1943, in a short, nasty fight in which almost the whole Japanese garrison of 2,350 were casualties.

At the southern end, the major Japanese base lay at Rabaul on New Britain Island. General MacArthur and a mixed American-Australian force were to advance from their base at Port Moresby and fight their way through the steaming jungles along the northern New Guinea coast. On the other side of Rabaul, Admiral William F. "Bull" Halsey's force was to take the islands of the northern Solomons, leaving the base flanked out on both sides.

MacArthur's men started struggling

The map shows the chief thrusts of the American counterattack in the Pacific. The vast distances made the supply problem one of the most difficult of the war.

MAP BY CAL SACKS

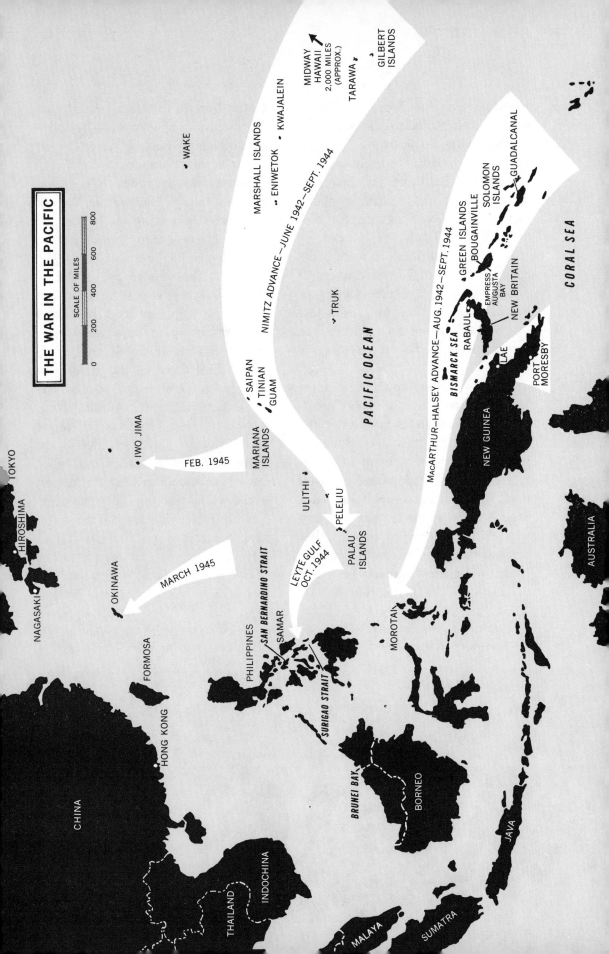

THE WAR IN THE PACIFIC

SCALE OF MILES

0   200   400   600   800

MIDWAY
HAWAII
2,000 MILES
(APPROX.)

TARAWA

GILBERT
ISLANDS

WAKE

MARSHALL ISLANDS

ENIWETOK   KWAJALEIN

NIMITZ ADVANCE—JUNE 1942—SEPT. 1944

TRUK

PACIFIC OCEAN

SAIPAN
TINIAN
GUAM

MARIANA
ISLANDS

IWO JIMA

FEB. 1945

ULITHI

PELELIU

PALAU
ISLANDS

LEYTE GULF
OCT. 1944

MacARTHUR–HALSEY ADVANCE—AUG. 1942—SEPT. 1944

BISMARCK SEA

RABAUL

NEW BRITAIN

EMPRESS
AUGUSTA
BAY

BOUGAINVILLE

GREEN ISLANDS

SOLOMON
ISLANDS

GUADALCANAL

CORAL SEA

LAE

PORT
MORESBY

NEW GUINEA

MOROTAI

AUSTRALIA

OKINAWA

MARCH 1945

NAGASAKI

HIROSHIMA

TOKYO

FORMOSA

HONG KONG

CHINA

PHILIPPINES

SAN BERNARDINO STRAIT

SAMAR

SURIGAO STRAIT

BRUNEI BAY

BORNEO

INDOCHINA

THAILAND

MALAYA

SUMATRA

JAVA

toward Lae in January, 1943. Tokyo promptly attempted to reinforce New Guinea with 7,000 troops in eight transports convoyed by eight destroyers. In the Battle of the Bismarck Sea, American and Australian planes caught the convoy and destroyed it with the loss of only five planes.

Even without reinforcements, the Japanese managed to keep MacArthur out of Lae until September. The jungle was their ally; the Americans lost nearly as many men to combat fatigue and malaria as they did to enemy bullets.

Working his way up the Solomons' ladder, Halsey ran into similar resistance from the island garrisons and the Japanese surface fleet. At Bougainville, the Americans attempted no direct assault on the Japanese garrison of 60,000 men, but simply grabbed a beachhead at Empress Augusta Bay with enough room for airfields that could be used against the rest of the island and against Rabaul itself, 210 miles away. Then, in February, 1944,

Halsey hopped to Green Island, completely cutting off Rabaul on its northern flank and putting American air power within 120 miles.

MacArthur, meanwhile, was leapfrogging along the northern New Guinea coast, making new landings to bypass heavy enemy concentrations in the jungle. By the end of May, 1944, he was at the western end of the island, the second largest in the world. Rabaul was finished as a base, and 135,000 Japanese troops were hopelessly stranded in the South Pacific.

The third prong of the attack was designed to seize enemy-held islands in the Central Pacific. Admiral Nimitz was in charge, and his first target was Tarawa, a tiny coral atoll in the Gilbert Islands. It turned out to be one of the bloodiest pieces of terrain in the whole war for the Americans. The admiral commanding the 4,000 Japanese troops on the island had fortified it heavily and boasted that it could not be taken with a million men. On November 21, the Second

Having received treatment from hospital corpsmen on the beach on D-Day, a wounded man is carried to a boat that will take him to a ship's sick bay.

Marine Division went ashore, after a naval and air bombardment, to see if the admiral was right. At first it seemed he was. Landing craft grounded on coral reefs, leaving the marines with 700 yards of Pacific to wade through to get ashore. The entire distance was under enemy fire because the heavy bunkers on the island had survived most of the bombardment. By the next morning, the marines had two small beachheads and one of their commanders messaged, "Our casualties heavy. Enemy casualties unknown. Situation: We are winning." After four days, they did win, but it cost nearly 1,000 dead and over 2,000 wounded. The experience was costly, but it taught Nimitz to insist on heavier bombardments and better landing craft in future operations. With lighter casualties, the marines and the army went on to take Kwajalein and Eniwetok in the Marshalls and Japan's outer barrier was gone.

The end of Fortress Europe

As 1944 opened in Europe, everyone knew what was coming. This was to be the year of the long-awaited cross-channel invasion for which British, American, Canadian, and French forces had prepared in England. Before it began, however, there was some unfinished business in Italy. "Smiling Albert" Kesselring had the Allies stalled in the mud along a line anchored on the fortress height of Monte Cassino. The decision was to outflank Kesselring by making a new

The Allied commander for the invasion of Europe was General Dwight D. Eisenhower.

landing behind him and cause him to pull back or be trapped between two forces. The spot chosen was Anzio, a small resort town in peacetime, just south of Rome. A force of 70,000 Americans and British got ashore easily on January 22, but failed to move inland quickly enough. The agile Kesselring held at Cassino and moved his reserves onto the hills above the beachhead. Far from threatening the Germans, the landing force just managed to hold on against hard counterattacks and then had to huddle in its dugouts, drummed by artillery fire from above. Not until May did the Fifth and Eighth Armies break through at Cassino, link up with the beachhead troops, and enter Rome, which the Germans had declared an open city and left, undamaged, on June 4.

Two days later—June 6, 1944—the

Hedgerows on embankments turned many Normandy fields into enemy forts that gave the American infantry stubborn resistance as it struggled to advance.

invasion of France finally came. In weather far from perfect, 150,000 men, 5,000 ships, and 12,000 planes set out over the choppy English Channel for the assault that was to free Europe. Just after midnight, British and American paratroopers started dropping behind the invasion beaches, and at 6:30 the seaborne forces went ashore at a series of points between Cherbourg and Le Havre. The paratroops and glider troops came down badly scattered and took heavy casualties. On Omaha Beach, two American divisions ran into ferocious opposition from a crack German unit stationed there, unknown to Allied intelligence, on anti-invasion maneuvers. The Canadians had hard fighting on Juno Beach, but in general the operation went well there, with casualties considerably lighter than had been feared.

Cherbourg was taken before the end of June, but breaking out of the beachhead proved a tough, slogging job with the British bogged down in front of Caen. Yet they tied up much of the German armor as the Americans pushed toward St. Lo through farmland where each small field was surrounded by an earthen bank and hedgerow that turned it into a little fort. It was near the end of July before the two forces had achieved their objectives. On July 26, the American First Army, aided by heavy bombing ahead of it, punched a clean hole through the German lines south of St. Lo and General Patton's tanks went roaring through to loop around toward Argentan, where they joined the Canadians and trapped most of two German armies. To add to the enemy's plight, on August 15, the American Seventh Army landed on the French Riviera against light resistance and drove rapidly north.

The map shows the assaults that finally destroyed the Third Reich. The tide turned in the fall of 1942, when the Nazi offensives failed in Russia and North Africa.

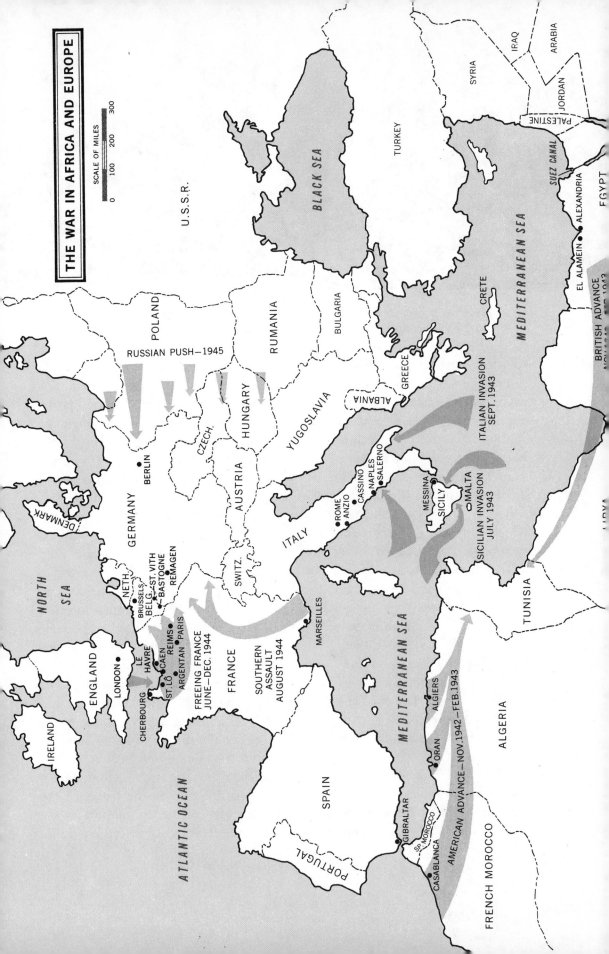

This is a typical field-dressing station set up just behind the front in a ruined village church. From here, stretcher cases moved to the rear in jeeps.

Hitler's men streamed back to the Siegfried Line, a defense position just outside Germany itself. Paris was free after four years, and General Charles de Gaulle arrived during the three-day spree of jubilation.

On the Allied left flank, the English and Canadians also moved swiftly and were in Brussels and Antwerp, Belgium, by early September. Then enemy resistance stiffened. Montgomery tried to outflank the Siegfried Line by dropping one British and two American airborne divisions north of it and then breaking through with a British army to support them. The breakthrough failed, and the paratroopers had to fight their way back with heavy losses. The conflict settled down to hard fighting for small gains in increasingly bitter weather.

Hitler's last gasp

With the Russians driving in on him from the east, Hitler resolved to stake almost his total available re-serve in a final effort against the Allied ring in the west. If the attack could recapture the Channel ports, the Americans and British might be discouraged enough, he thought, to make a separate peace. The drive would be made in the Ardennes, a thinly held sector where four American divisions were occupying a 90-mile stretch of front. It was hoped that bad winter weather would keep Allied air power on the ground. To do the job, a force of 250,000 men and 2,000 tanks was scraped together and assembled in the greatest secrecy. On December 16, the startled Americans saw them come rolling forward through an early morning fog. The front collapsed, and before it could be reestablished, the Nazis had rolled through the snow to make a bulge 45 miles wide and 65 miles deep.

The Allied defense firmed, then began to drive in on the flanks of the bulge with strong air support as the weather cleared. By the end of January, the lines were right back where they had been when the fight started, and all Hitler had to show for the Battle of the Bulge were 90,000 casualties.

The death of the Third Reich

There was still fierce fighting ahead, even against the boys and old men Hitler now had to use to eke out his forces, but by mid-March the Allies were on the Rhine and over it at Remagen, where a bridge was taken before it could be destroyed. Then Montgomery got six divisions across in a combined paratroop and ground attack. Suddenly everybody was moving forward, the Ruhr was encircled, and 325,000 German troops surrendered. Through April, the Allies converged on Berlin from east and west. On April 28, Mussolini was shot by Italian partisans, and on April 30, Hitler committed suicide. Two days later, the Russian army entered Berlin. On May 7, General Alfred Jodl, representing what German government there was, signed an unconditional surrender in Eisenhower's headquarters at Reims. After almost six years, the war in Europe was at an end.

Closing in in the Pacific

The time had come for the assault on the islands close to Japan, and in June, 1944, Commander of the Pacific Fleet Nimitz sent Admiral Spruance after the key island of Saipan in the Marianas. Once it was taken, airfields could be built there from which the new B-29 bombers could attack Japan itself. Spruance had 77,000 men and the Japanese

Allied bombers regularly worked over German cities to reduce their war production capacities. Below are the ruins of Nuremberg after six years of war.

commander had 32,000, but the terrain was rugged and its defenders were stubborn. They fought for nearly a month, with the last Japanese units dying in wild banzai charges that piled in on American positions until marine and army artillerymen were firing with their fuses set on zero.

On June 19, the Japanese sent a carrier force down in an attempt to drive off the Americans. In the three-day air battle that followed, they lost over 300 planes and three carriers; the Americans lost only 23 Hellcat fighters. The score on land was not nearly so favorable; there were over 16,000 American casualties before the island was secured and the B-29s had their base. Guam and Tinian were captured after more heavy fighting, and the conquest of the Marianas was complete.

Farther south, MacArthur's men landed on Morotai Island, thus flanking the Philippines on that side, and Halsey took Peleliu in the Palau Islands after the bitterest kind of fighting. Now MacArthur could make good his promise to return to the Philippines.

The end of the Japanese navy

MacArthur was to land at Leyte Gulf on Leyte Island. To support him, there were two fleets—Halsey's Third, with the fast carriers to deal with any intervention by the Japanese navy, and Admiral Thomas Kinkaid's Seventh to provide fire support for the ground troops. Many of Kinkaid's battleships had been raised from the mud at Pearl Harbor where the raid that started the war had left them, and their moment of vengeance was now at hand.

To counter the landing, the Japanese had devised a complex and crafty plan. They had some carriers left, but a

On Saipan, 25,000 of the 32,000 Japanese defenders died, the last of them in wild banzai charges. Here some of the dead lie near an American tank.

*Here, at the Japanese surrender, are three of the architects of victory in
the Pacific: Commander in Chief of the Pacific Fleet Admiral Chester W. Nimitz,
General Douglas MacArthur (right), and behind him Admiral William Halsey.*

great shortage of good pilots. These
ships would be dangled off the northern end of the Philippines in the virtual certainty that Halsey would run
north to get them and leave the transports and landing craft in Leyte Gulf
uncovered. To annihilate these de-
fenseless vessels and defeat the invasion, two forces were prepared. One
was to fuel at Brunei Bay in Borneo,
then run north and come through San
Bernardino Strait north of Samar. It
would comprise the best of the Japanese battleships and cruisers and be
more than a match for Kinkaid's old-
timers. A smaller surface force, based
in Japan, was to run through Surigao
Strait south of Leyte and take care
of any vessels that might evade Admiral Takeo Kurita's main force.

On October 20, 1944, MacArthur
landed and announced, "People of the
Philippines, I have returned." The infantry started its drive to retake the
islands, and then, on October 23, the
greatest sea battle in history began.

This was the war's most famous photograph —the marine flag-raising on Iwo Jima.

The American submarines *Darter* and *Dace* found Kurita steaming north, sank two of his cruisers, and gave Halsey his position. Through October 24, Halsey's planes kept after Kurita and sank one of the world's two largest battleships, *Musashi,* with her 18-inch guns. Just at last light, Halsey received a report from a scout plane that Kurita was turning back from the western end of San Bernardino Strait. Satisfied that his opponent had had enough, Halsey turned and raced north to hit the Japanese carriers.

During the night, the Japanese southern force started through Surigao Strait in column and Kinkaid had them spotted. At the eastern end, he had his old battlewagons in line and waiting in the classic surface-navy tactical position: He was the crossbar on the enemy T. The Japanese saved only one destroyer out of all the ships that went into the strait.

So far, so good, but Kinkaid's force had used up most of its ammunition, and with Halsey up north, Kurita turned back and into San Bernardino Strait. Urging his force to "Advance, counting on divine assistance," he ran through the strait at night, a superb piece of navigation, and at dawn was ready to fall upon the transports, which were covered by only a small force of light carriers, three destroyers, and four little destroyer escorts. Kurita had four battleships—one the 18-inch *Yamato*—seven cruisers, and a screen of destroyers. Admiral C.A.F. Sprague, commanding the north carrier group, could only run south with his thin-skinned vessels, try to recover his aircraft—which were supporting ground troops—and get them back into the air with armor-piercing bombs. The destroyers and the destroyer escorts had to cover the retreat as best they could with torpedoes and smoke. In one of the great actions in American naval history, the seven little ships sacrificed themselves to stall the Japanese giants. Three were sunk and the others were riddled, but they stayed alive long enough for Sprague to get his planes off against the attacker. Incredibly, with victory in his hands, Kurita turned and ran back through the straits. He had heard of the disaster at Surigao and he thought he was up against much greater forces than he was, but his decision can only be recorded as one of the great blunders of the war. Up north, Halsey had knocked out four enemy carriers and the last great counterattack had failed.

It took until June, 1945, to clear the Philippines fully, but from that day on, the issue was never really in doubt. Long before that, on February 19, 1945, marines had gone ashore on the little island of Iwo Jima—the object, to get an airfield from which fighter cover could go with the B-29s against Japan and provide a way station for damaged bombers coming back. Admiral Spruance plastered the island with everything he had, but the Japanese held out against the invaders for nearly a month. There were 25,000 casualties before the job was done, and the Marine Corps declared it the toughest engagement in their history.

The last battle

There remained only the island of Okinawa, just south of Japan and an ideal staging point for an invasion of the home islands. Army troops and marines went ashore on April 1, 1945,

To avoid the casualties it would cost to invade Japan, the atomic bomb was dropped on Hiroshima. Only this was left a mile from the center of the blast.

and it looked easy. A wily Japanese commander had pulled his forces back into the hills to escape the bombardment he knew the Americans would put on the landing beaches. It took until the end of June to clear the island, and in the process, the navy took its worst pounding since Pearl Harbor. The Japanese turned to suicide pilots —kamikazes. They were half-trained, sworn to die, and flying anything that could be got off the ground. They did not even try to bomb the American ships from the air; the bomb-ladened planes simply flew straight into their targets—planes, bombs, and pilots vanishing in a last glorious blast for homeland and emperor. The navy had 36 ships sunk and 368 damaged, and back in Washington, government officials wondered how much higher the price might be when Japan itself was invaded. There was still a Japanese army of 2,500,000 men, and President Harry S. Truman—succeeding Franklin D. Roosevelt, who had died in April—pondered a bitter decision.

The B-29s had lacerated Japan, but there was still no sign of surrender. In 1939, Dr. Albert Einstein had written Roosevelt about the possibility of building an atomic bomb. It was now ready—a weapon, as President Truman told Joseph Stalin at the Potsdam Conference, "the like of which has never been seen on this earth." It was estimated that half a million American lives could be saved if the bomb could knock Japan out of the war. Truman decided to use it, and on August 6, 1945, a B-29 named *Enola Gay,* piloted by Colonel Paul Tibbets, was over the Japanese city of Hiroshima, population 343,000.

On the blinding light and the mushroom cloud that followed, the crew of the plane could make only one comment: "My God."

Something like 120,000 people were killed, obliterated, or wounded.

Three days later, a second bomb was dropped on Nagasaki. Again there was the great fireball and the huge casualties. On August 14, the Japanese Supreme War Council decided that the time had come to surrender. Fanatics still resisted, but the next day, the emperor himself went on the radio and told his people that the war was over.

On September 2, 1945, an American fleet steamed into Tokyo Bay, and while planes flew fighter cover overhead, the surrender papers were signed on deck of the battleship U.S.S. *Missouri.*

A total of some 17,000,000 servicemen on both sides had died. There can be no exact count of the number of civilian dead, but an estimate is 18,-000,000. American military casualties alone had been 1,078,674. Now the nation faced the peace uneasily, with a new President, with the question of whether the economy could absorb 15,000,000 men and women returning from service, and signs aplenty that America's wartime ally, Russia, would be no ally or even a friend in the postwar world.

UNITED NATIONS

THE UNITED NATIONS

The expression "United Nations" was first used officially in a declaration made on January 1, 1942, in which 26 nations pledged themselves to carry on the war against the Axis until the finish. (The 26 leaders, plus General Charles de Gaulle, who seemed most likely to be the future leader of France, are shown on the following pages.) The charter was drawn up at the San Francisco Conference of 1945, and in that year the U.N. became a reality, with 51 member nations. If it has not brought the universal peace that some hoped it would, it has a considerable body of achievement to its credit. Today, delegates from almost 160 nations pour out millions of words a year at its meetings; the talk is often wearisome, but as Winston Churchill said, "Jaw, jaw, jaw is better than war, war, war." In Korea, the U.N. stood up to naked aggression far better than the old League of Nations ever did. It played a powerful role in settling the Suez crisis of 1956 and eight years later sent forces to maintain peace on the troubled island of Cyprus. The U.N.'s intervention in the Congo was one of the most important events in the life of that unhappy nation. As the U.N. has grown to more than triple its original membership, there has been a significant change in the balance of power. In the early days, the United States and its allies could muster a slight edge over the Soviet bloc on most issues. Today, the Afro-Asian bloc—many of its members new, small countries—has the votes in the General Assembly to overrule the supporters of either of the world's two great atomic powers. The police actions of the U.N. have been the most widely reported; in this portfolio the emphasis is on its nonmilitary activities.

THE UNITED NATIONS...FOR WAR AND FOR PEACE

A FANCIFUL ASSEMBLAGE OF THE HEADS OF STATE OF THE UNITED NATIONS
PAINTED IN 1942 BY MIGUEL COVARRUBIAS
IN THE BEST CARICATURING TRADITION OF THE FREE PRESS OF THE FREE WORLD

1 King George II of Greece
2 Grand Duchess Charlotte of the Grand Duchy of Luxembourg
3 Mackenzie King, Prime Minister of Canada
4 Generalissimo Chiang Kai-shek of China
5 Franklin D. Roosevelt, President of the United States of America
6 Winston Churchill, Prime Minister of the United Kingdom of Great Britain and Northern Ireland
7 Joseph Stalin, Chairman of the Council of People's Commissars of the Union of Soviet Socialist Republics
8 Queen Wilhelmina of the Netherlands
9 General Tiburcio Carias Andino, President of Honduras
10 King Haakon VII of Norway
11 King Peter II of Yugoslavia
12 John Curtin, Prime Minister of Australia
13 Peter Fraser, Prime Minister of New Zealand
14 General Wladyslaw Sikorski, Prime Minister of Poland
15 Hubert Pierlot, Prime Minister of Belgium
16 Eduard Benes, President of the Czechoslovak Republic
17 General Jan C. Smuts, Prime Minister of the Union of South Africa
18 Fulgencio Batista, President of Cuba
19 General Anastasio Somoza, President of Nicaragua
20 The Marquis of Linlithgow, Viceroy of India
21 Elie Lescot, President of Haiti
22 Ricardo Adolfo de la Guardia, President of Panama
23 Dr. Manuel de Jesus Troncoso de la Concha, President of the Dominican Republic
24 Dr. Rafael Angel Calderon Guardia, President of Costa Rica
25 General Maximiliano H. Martinez, President of El Salvador
26 General Jorge Ubico Castañeda, President of Guatemala
27 General Charles de Gaulle of the Free French

THE HOME OFFICE

The home of the United Nations is at the edge of New York City's East River. The lower building in the foreground (left) houses the General Assembly and the special councils. The taller shaft to the rear, with glass sides and marble ends, is the office building for the Secretariat—the permanent professional staff of the organization. Various nations have contributed ornamentation; paradoxically, the muscular figure beating his sword into a plowshare (right) is a gift of the bellicose Soviet bloc. When the General Assembly is in session, flags of all members nations are displayed. These meetings begin each September and, after a midwinter break, continue into March or April.

DICK HANLEY, PHOTO RESEARCHERS

The colorful flags on the following pages show the tremendous growth in the number of member nations since the U.N. General Assembly first met in London in January, 1946, with 51 members.

1. Afghanistan	35. Congo	64. Guinea-Bissau	99. Mozambique	131. South Africa
2. Albania	36. Costa Rica	65. Guyana	100. Nepal	132. Spain
3. Algeria	37. Côte D'Ivoire	66. Haiti	101. Netherlands	133. Sri Lanka
4. Angola	38. Cuba	67. Honduras	102. New Zealand	134. Sudan
5. Antigua	39. Cyprus	68. Hungary	103. Nicaragua	135. Suriname
6. Argentina	40. Czechoslovakia	69. Iceland	104. Niger	136. Swaziland
7. Australia	41. Democratic	70. India	105. Nigeria	137. Sweden
8. Austria	Kampuchea	71. Indonesia	106. Norway	138. Syria
9. Bahamas	42. Democratic	72. Iran	107. Oman	139. Thailand
10. Bahrain	Yemen	73. Iraq	108. Pakistan	140. Togo
11. Bangladesh	43. Denmark	74. Ireland	109. Panama	141. Trinidad-
12. Barbados	44. Djibouti	75. Israel	110. Papua New	Tobago
13. Belgium	45. Dominica	76. Italy	Guinea	142. Tunisia
14. Belize	46. Dominican	77. Jamaica	111. Paraguay	143. Turkey
15. Benin	Republic	78. Japan	112. Peru	144. Uganda
16. Bhutan	47. Ecuador	79. Jordan	113. Philippines	145. Ukraine
17. Bolivia	48. Egypt	80. Kenya	114. Poland	146. Union of Soviet
18. Botswana	49. El Salvador	81. Kuwait	115. Portugal	Socialist
19. Brazil	50. Equatorial Guinea	82. Laos	116. Qatar	Republics
20. Brunei	51. Ethiopia	83. Lebanon	117. Romania	147. United Arab
21. Bulgaria	52. Fiji	84. Lesotho	118. Rwanda	Emirates
22. Burkina Faso	53. Finland	85. Liberia	119. St. Christopher	148. United
23. Burma	54. France	86. Libya	and Nevis	Kingdom
24. Burundi	55. Gabon	87. Luxembourg	120. St. Lucia	149. United Republic
25. Byelorussian SSR	56. Gambia	88. Madagascar	121. St. Vincent	of Tanzania
26. Cameroon	57. German	89. Malawi	122. Samoa	150. United States
27. Canada	Democratic	90. Malaysia	123. Sao Tomé and	151. Uruguay
28. Cape Verde	Republic	91. Maldives	Principé	152. Vanuatu
29. Central African	58. German Federal	92. Mali	124. Saudi Arabia	153. Venezuela
Republic	Republic	93. Malta	125. Senegal	154. Viet Nam
30. Chad	59. Ghana	94. Mauritania	126. Seychelles	155. Yemen
31. Chile	60. Greece	95. Mauritius	127. Sierra Leone	156. Yugoslavia
32. China	61. Grenada	96. Mexico	128. Singapore	157. Zaire
33. Colombia	62. Guatemala	97. Mongolia	129. Solomons	158. Zambia
34. Comoros	63. Guinea	98. Morocco	130. Somalia	159. Zimbabwe

POSTER FROM THE UNITED NATIONS GIFT SHOP

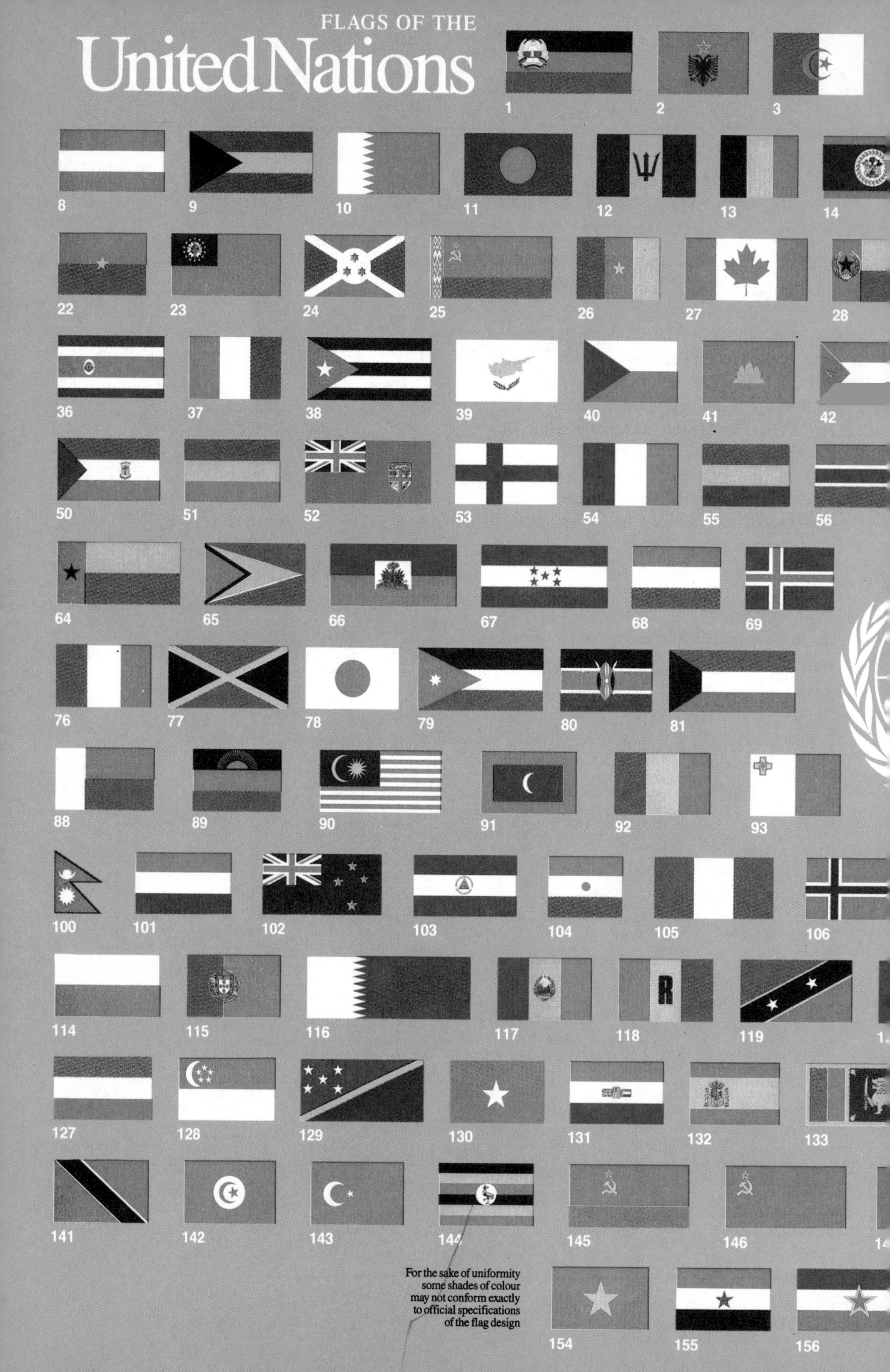

FLAGS OF THE
United Nations

1
2
3

8
9
10
11
12
13
14

22
23
24
25
26
27
28

36
37
38
39
40
41
42

50
51
52
53
54
55
56

64
65
66
67
68
69

76
77
78
79
80
81

88
89
90
91
92
93

100
101
102
103
104
105
106

114
115
116
117
118
119
1.

127
128
129
130
131
132
133

141
142
143
144
145
146
14

For the sake of uniformity
some shades of colour
may not conform exactly
to official specifications
of the flag design

154
155
156

DRAPEAUX DES

Nations Unies

5
6
7

16 17 18 19 20 21
30 31 32 33 34 35
44 45 46 47 48 49
58 59 60 61 62 63
70 71 72 73 74 75
82 83 84 85 86 87
94 95 96 97 98 99
108 109 110 111 112 113
121 122 123 124 125 126
135 136 137 138 139 140
148 149 150 151 152 153

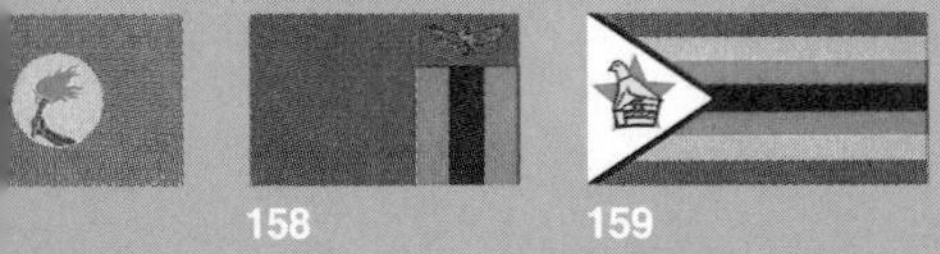

158
159

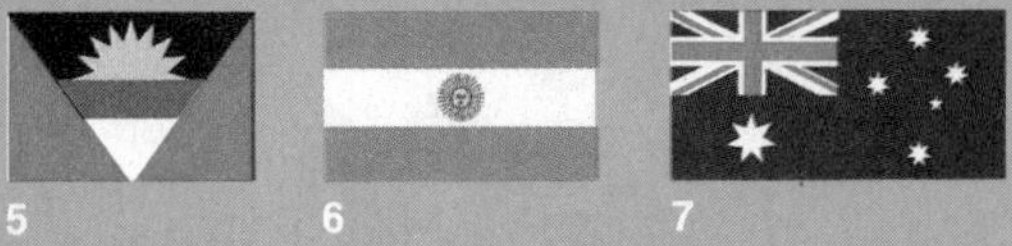

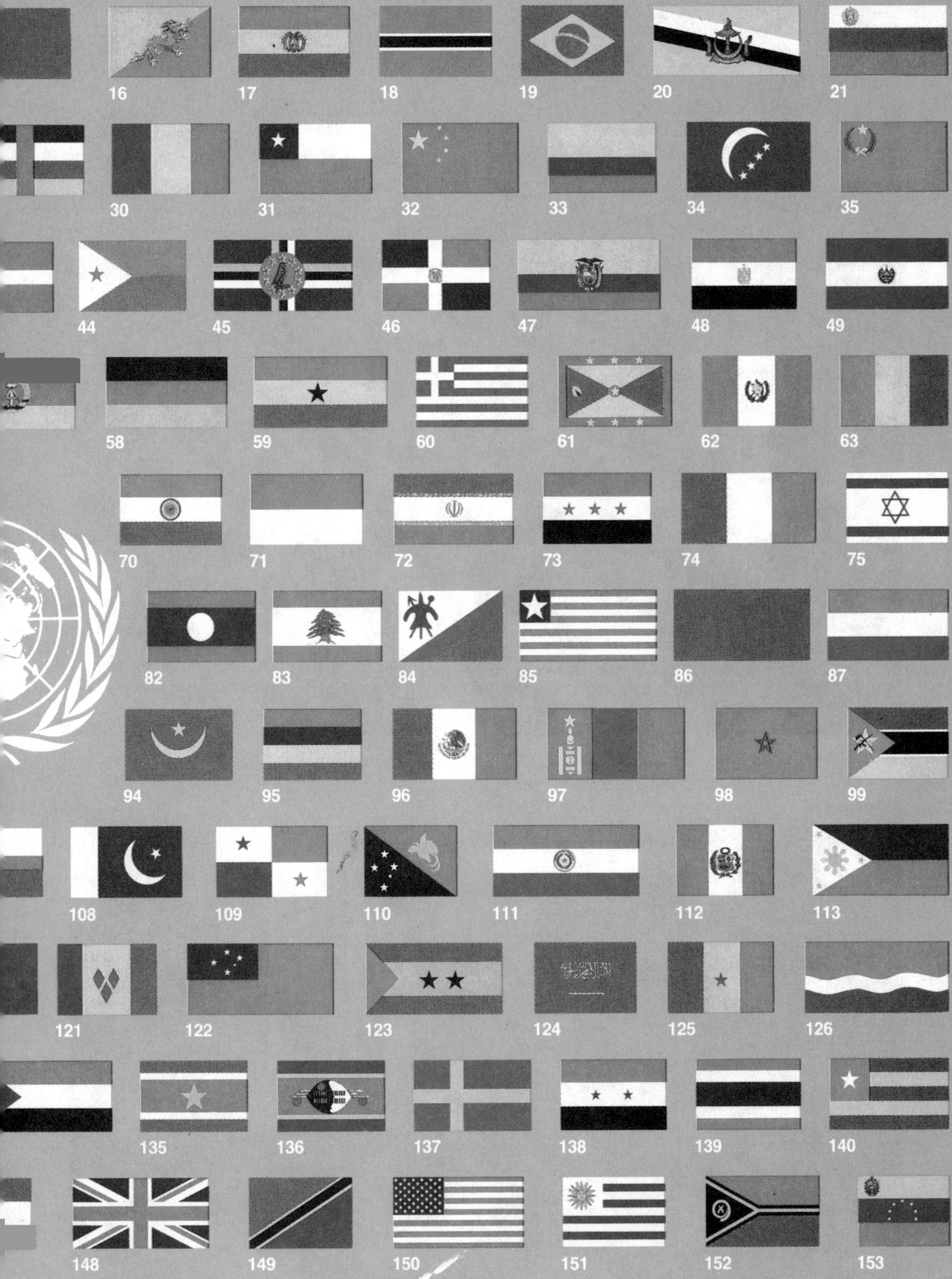

Par souci d'uniformité, certaines nuances de couleurs peuvent ne pas correspondre exactement aux caractéristiques officielles des drapeaux

THE HEART

When the General Assembly is in session, the Secretary-General and his staff members sit at the far right (above) under the great seal. At the left is one of the two large Fernand Leger murals that decorate the chamber. The delegates (right) have a choice of hearing a speech translated into Arabic, Chinese, English, French, Russian, or Spanish. The same simultaneous translation takes place in the Security Council (left), where the mural is a gift to the U.N. from Norway. Only the five permanent members of the Security Council have the veto power.

UNITED NATIONS

THE UNITED NATIONS

BRANCH OFFICES

The U.N. ranges far from New York City. The International Court of Justice sits at The Hague in the Netherlands (above). Its 15 judges are elected by the Security Council and the General Assembly; care is taken to see that all the leading legal systems of the world are represented. The old League of Nations building at Geneva (right, above) contains many of the U.N. European offices. Of all the U.N. multinational military efforts, intervention in Korea was the greatest. Troops (right) sent by 16 nations took part in the struggle, suffering 400,000 casualties.

WIDE WORLD

THE UNITED NATIONS

IN NEWEST AFRICA

An important part of the U.N. activities has been to assist nations that have just attained independence or are about to do so. Above, children celebrate the 1962 creation of the Republic of Rwanda, once part of the territory—Ruanda-Urundi—administered by Belgium for the Trusteeship Council. In the Congo, the U.N. faced a hornet's nest of problems, which took years to solve. Secretary-General Dag Hammarskjold died in an air crash in Africa while trying to resolve some of them. One problem was displaced natives, whom the U.N. fed and then sent back to their own lands. At the right, members of the Baluba tribe crowd around an official while he announces over a loud-speaker those who are about to be taken home.

MEDICAL AID

UNICEF—the United Nations Children's Fund—is an integral part of the U.N., created in 1946 by the General Assembly. Founded originally to bring immediate aid to child victims of World War II, its activities have been expanded to take in the long-term needs of children. Working particularly in underdeveloped areas, it deals in both direct disease control and educational programs aimed at better child and maternity care. At the left, a medical team in Morocco examines children for trachoma, which can cause blindness. At the right, doctors in Indonesia examine for yaws, and below, powdered milk is being distributed to Masai tribesmen in Kenya.

UNICEF

UNICEF

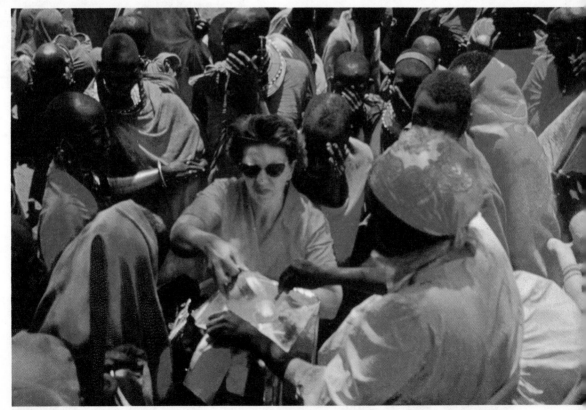

UNITED NATIONS

BOOKS AND CLASSES

The intergovernmental agencies related to the United Nations cooperate with the U.N. but are not directly a part of it. Indeed, some of them—like the International Telecommunications Union, which was founded in 1865—existed long before the U.N. itself. Their activities are financed by the member governments, but the Administrative Committee on Coordination at the U.N. helps them interrelate their work. At right, a library sponsored by UNESCO —the United Nations Educational, Scientific and Cultural Organization—has just arrived in a Thailand village. Below, Peruvian villagers vote on a proposition put by a UNESCO rural-education expert. He trains them not only in technical skills, but helps them gain practical experience in self-government at the local level. Below, right, a Food and Agricultural Organization instructor from the Netherlands teaches Congolese farmers how to use a tractor at a school in the capital city of Kinshasa.

ALL: UNITED NATIONS

1327

NEW FRONTIERS

In addition to its medical and instructional programs, the U.N. also offers economic assistance, both direct and indirect. The yarn merchant at the left is an Arab refugee living in the Gaza Strip whom the U.N. Relief and Works Agency helped set up in business. The aqueduct below is part of a Japanese irrigation project, which was helped by a World Bank loan of nearly $5,000,000. The aqueduct not only brings new acres under cultivation to enlarge Japan's food supply, but it also provides, for the first time, adequate drinking water for many small villages in the area. The U.N. provides help, too, for farmers learning how best to use new agricultural projects like the irrigation canal at the right in Pakistan.

ALL: UNITED NATIONS

Today the U.N. still fights, as its charter specifies, "to save succeeding generations from th

courge of war . . . to promote social progress and better standards of life in larger freedom."

THE HOME AND DIPLOMATIC FRONTS

In a conflict that had lasted six years, the dictators Hitler, Mussolini, and Tojo had been defeated by the combined forces of Churchill, Roosevelt, and Stalin. Throughout, Roosevelt and Churchill had conferred often—starting with the Atlantic Charter meeting in 1941. They met again at Casablanca in January, 1943, with Charles de Gaulle present, and in November at Cairo along with Chiang Kai-shek of China. Finally, later in November, the Big Three met together for the first time at Teheran, Iran. The conference was marked by military planning, a reaffirmation of the fact that the Allies planned a world organization after the war, and a vast number of pronouncements of goodfellowship spurred on by endless toasts.

Then in February, 1945, with the conflict drawing to an end, the Big Three met again, this time at the Russian Black Sea resort of Yalta, for the

The Big Three meet at Yalta with Churchill, Roosevelt, and Stalin. Sir Anthony Eden, Edward R. Stettinius, Jr., Sir Alexander Cadogan, Vyacheslav Molotov, and Averell Harriman are behind them. Yalta became the most controversial wartime conference.

most controversial gathering of the war. In the years following, Roosevelt would be accused of being duped.

The facts are somewhat less melodramatic. It would be well to realize Roosevelt's aims at Yalta. He wanted Russia to enter the war against Japan at a time when that nation was still strong and an invasion of the Japanese home islands threatened untold casualties. Like Woodrow Wilson before him, he wanted a postwar association of nations and, like Wilson, he was willing to make certain concessions to get it.

What was actually done at Yalta? A date was set for the San Francisco conference that would charter the United Nations. Russia would enter the war against Japan, but her entry had a big price tag on it: She was to get back all the territory she had lost to Japan in the Russo-Japanese War and was also to have the Kurile Islands, which had always been Japanese. The autonomy of the Mongolian People's Republic, which had existed since 1924, was recognized, although China still claimed the area as the Chinese province of Outer Mongolia. Chiang Kai-shek

In this Persian miniature commemorating the Teheran Conference, Stalin, Churchill, Roosevelt, and Chiang (left to right) hunt down Mussolini, Hitler, and Tojo. The artist, Haji Musavirel Mulk, made one for Churchill, one for F.D.R.

was not informed, and Roosevelt was assigned to break the news to him. In Eastern Europe, some minor adjustments were made in the Polish-Russian border, but it remained basically as it was established by the Allies after World War I.

The most bitterly contested decision concerned the Polish government. The Russians, in military occupation of Poland, naturally favored a group that was Communist-oriented. The British and Americans favored another Polish government, in exile in London. It was agreed that the Russian-backed group should be enlarged to include some of the Londoners, and the eventual government chosen by the Poles themselves in a free election. It can certainly be said that Roosevelt misread Stalin badly if he thought the dictator would ever permit truly free elections in a Russian-occupied country.

Considering the time at which the Yalta Conference was held, the agreements contained some good judgment and some bad. After the war, when quarreling among recent allies disillusioned the free world, it was much easier, with hindsight, to show up some of the decisions for the mistakes they were and to blame those who made them.

The final great conference of the war was held at Potsdam, Germany, in July, 1945. One member of the Big Three was new; Roosevelt was dead and Harry S. Truman had replaced him. Churchill represented England at first, but before the end, he had been voted out of office and replaced by Labor Prime Minister Clement R. Attlee. The conference was largely concerned with Stalin's demanding and getting huge reparations from Germany in return for the enormous damage his nation had suffered.

The home front

Although the United States raised an armed force of unprecedented size, less than 15% of the population was actually in uniform. For most people, the war was something one read about, heard about on the radio, or saw either in heavily edited or censored newsreels or in unrealistic mov-

The Potsdam Conference ended with a new team representing the Allies—Clement R. Atlee, Harry S. Truman, and Joseph Stalin. Behind them are Admiral William D. Leahy, Britain's Ernest Bevin, James F. Byrnes, and Vyacheslav Molotov.

A wartime poster lauds the support of the women at home who went to work in factories to help keep the supply lines filled.

ies in which handfuls of Americans decimated three times as many Japanese. There actually were merchant-ship sinkings within sight of East Coast residents and the Japanese did attempt to set fire to West Coast forests, but no bombs fell on American soil. Most citizens assumed, in one way or another, the role of the man behind the man behind the gun. Yet nearly everyone was personally involved, usually through a father, son, daughter, or other relative in service. Some worked in defense industries, others volunteered for a wide vari-

ety of duties, including those of air-raid wardens, auxiliary firemen, and aircraft-warning watchers, and the thankless jobs of ration-board clerk or draft-board member.

Although Selective Service included men between 45 and 65, with the idea of a possible labor draft, no such legislation was necessary. American labor produced as never before and with a minimum of complaint. The picture, however, was not completely unmarred by strikes. Part of the trouble came from antilabor legislation passed by Congress, which helped to induce just what it tried to avoid. Workers wanted to retain all the gains they had made during the early days of the New Deal, and they feared that restrictions imposed in wartime might be kept in force afterward.

In June, 1943, apprehensive Congressmen passed the War Labor Disputes Act over Roosevelt's veto. It empowered the President to take over any industry threatened by stoppage through labor disputes. The Congressmen were unduly jittery. The loss of man-hours through strikes during the war was less than from absenteeism in the same businesses or industries in peacetime.

The vast war was expensive, costing the United States $330,500,000,000 compared to $41,755,000,000 for its predecessor in 1917–18. Industrial mobilization followed the pattern worked out in the later stages of World War I. The highest authority was the War Production Board, and workers came under the War Manpower Commission. Other agencies, such as the War Shipping Administration, the War Food Administration, and the Foreign Economic Administration, guided and correlated the nation's resources.

In some cases there was little to conserve or allocate. Raw rubber, for example, was almost nonexistent, as Japan controlled about 90% of the world's supply shortly after Pearl Harbor. The United States had less than a year's supply at the outbreak of hostilities. This was impressed sharply on the people at home when in January, 1942, a strict rationing of tires and other rubber products was put in force. The ever-present sight of balding tires was a constant reminder to automobile-conscious America that a real crisis was at hand. Gasoline rationing and a national speed limit of 35 miles an hour underscored it.

Production problems of all kinds faced the nation, but one of the most important was coordination as automobile and threshing-machine factories turned to producing tanks and airplanes.

After some preliminary difficulties, the job went well. A Congressional watchdog committee headed by Senator Harry S. Truman (Democrat, Missouri) assumed the task of shepherding the laggards, investigating charges of excess profits, and cutting away obstacles that impeded production schedules. In the process, it made such a name for its chairman that he

The driver of a barouche in New York City's Central Park gets a horse laugh with a newspaper announcing gas rationing.

was the Democratic nominee for Vice-President in the 1944 elections.

By 1942, American war production was equal to that of the Axis powers, and by 1944 it far surpassed their combined effort. The various controls imposed on industry and the consumer would normally have been resented as socialistic, but in the emergency, most of those who stayed at home submitted to unusual disciplines with reasonably good grace.

Early in 1942, the Office of Price Administration was established to fix what it regarded as a fair price on food items and thus attempt to prevent runaway inflation. Early efforts to keep prices stable were only partly successful, and by the spring of 1943, Roosevelt was forced to issue his "hold the line" order that price-fixed almost every item in the economy. It was so effective that in the next two years, price rises were held to 2%. During the whole war, prices rose approximately 30%, an increase about half that of the 1914–18 period.

Materially, the American people sacrificed but did not suffer. Although the purchasing power of the dollar declined slightly due to inflation, the nation enjoyed full employment for the first time since the '20s.

The return of peace

Franklin D. Roosevelt died on April 12, 1945, after serving a little over 12 years in the White House. That evening the Vice-President, Harry S.

Truman, was sworn in as his successor. Just as Lincoln had died on an April day at the very climax of a successful war, so Roosevelt passed away in his moment of triumph. Truman, like Lincoln's successor Andrew Johnson before him, was faced with the thorny task of making the peace.

Truman, a crisp-speaking and sometimes jaunty Missourian, was better prepared for what lay ahead than many of his contemporaries knew. A story made the rounds that in the summer of 1944, Roosevelt revealed to a Washington figure that Truman was to be his running mate in the election that year. The recipient of the news is said to have replied, "Who the hell is Harry Truman?" Not everyone was so ill-informed. The new President had served in the Senate since 1934. His fairness and capacity for hard work had favorably impressed the public.

Still, America faced the peace led

Vice-President Truman, left, dines with F.D.R. at Warm Springs. His record as the head of the Senate watchdog committee on war production won him the job.

Franklin Roosevelt rides through Washington for the last time. The nation mourned as the President's body traveled from Georgia to Hyde Park, New York.

by a man inexperienced in the massive complexities of global affairs. The ancient territorial ambitions of Russia, now strengthened by an ideology that promised them eventual victory over the capitalistic West, were making themselves felt. Europe lay in ruins, and it was clear that the means to rebuild it would have to come largely from the United States. In Asia there was turmoil as nations threw off old colonial bonds, and even in 1945 there were signs of the gravest weaknesses in Chiang Kai-shek's government in China.

At home, the largest armed force that America had ever assembled had to be dispersed, and there were great pressures to do it rapidly. Both civilians and servicemen clamored for immediate demobilization. Early in 1946, there were riots among some troops abroad that did not think the government was moving fast enough. Goaded by such pressures, Congress cut the fighting forces as quickly as it could. The naysayers muttered direly about a "mature economy" and questioned whether jobs could be found for all those returning. The man in the White House and the people he led faced a future that threatened to be nearly as troublesome as the period through which they had just passed.

MAIN TEXT CONTINUES IN VOLUME 16

Gunner's mate second class Allen Heyn was one of the 10 men out of more than 700 aboard the cruiser U.S.S. Juneau who survived her sinking.

One Who Survived:
The Narrative of Allen Heyn

Day after day, the sun, the sea, and the sharks cut down the men who clung to a doughnut life raft, until on the ninth day a plane spotted the solitary survivor.

*O*f all those who have gone down to the sea in ships, few have lived to tell a more graphic story than Allen Clifton Heyn, gunner's mate second class, one of the 10 survivors of more than 700 men aboard the United States light cruiser* Juneau. *This special contribution is a transcript of a recorded wartime interview between Heyn and a naval interrogator, reproduced here with permission of the Navy Department. Except for some cuts and for a few slight alterations in wording in the interest of clarity, nothing has been changed.*

ALLEN HEYN'S STORY

LT. PORTER: Heyn, you were on the *Juneau* in Guadalcanal action; that was 13 November 1942, wasn't it?

ALLEN HEYN: Yes, sir.

LT. PORTER: What was your battle station?

HEYN: I was on the 1.1 on the fantail. [A light gun at the stern.]

LT. PORTER: What did you see of the action that night?

HEYN: We were in a column of ships and we went in, in between these Japanese ships, and we got word down from the bridge to stand by, that they would challenge the enemy. And it wasn't but a few minutes when everything just broke loose, flames and shots and gunfire all over. And they sent word all around to all the minor batteries like 1.1s and 20 millimeters [antiaircraft machine guns] not to fire because the tracers would give away our positions.

So we held our fire until the enemy knew where we were and the star shells [fired to illuminate or silhouette an enemy at night] lit us all up. Then we started firing, and you could see the Jap ships so close that you'd think you could almost throw something and hit them. So we just fired our smaller guns right into the topsides [superstructures] of their ships, trying to knock off some of the guns on their decks. That went on quite a while and the ship maneuvered around a lot.

I don't know whether they knew there was a fish [torpedo] coming or what, but all at once a fish hit. It must have hit up forward because it just seemed like the fish jumped out of the water.* And when it did, all of us fellows that were on the main deck, it stunned us like and knocked us down. The propellers didn't seem to turn for a few minutes. Sounded like they were jammed or something. The ship wouldn't steer, just seemed to skid through the water like. I don't know whether it was a Jap cruiser or what it was, but it was on the other side of us and it just seemed like we were going to run right into it and ram it, but we didn't, though.

The ship seemed to be out of control, and they passed the word around to cut some of the life rafts loose. There were four or five of these doughnut rafts stacked on top of each other on the main deck aft, and they were

*It struck the forward fireroom (Samuel Eliot Morison, *The Struggle for Guadalcanal, History of U.S. Naval Operations in World War II, Vol. V).*

secured, so two or three guys from the battle station where I was went up and cut them loose with a knife and come back.

After that, things started to quiet down a little. We got out of position and didn't see any more ships around us. The forward part of the ship seemed to be way down in the water and the fantail way up high. And we couldn't make very good speed. You could hear the things cracking underneath there—the propeller shafts and the rudder. They were bent or something.

It was beginning to get daylight by then, and we got out in the open sea again. The radars and things didn't work very good; they were all shot from the explosion. Then the lookouts picked up ships ahead. They signaled recognition signals, and we found out then it was some of our own task force.

It was the *San Francisco*, the *Buchanan*, and I don't know the name of the other can. The *San Francisco* sent over word to our ship asking for a doctor and some pharmacist's mates to come over and aid them. We only had two small motor launches on the davits and they were all torn away. So they [the *San Francisco*] sent a boat over, and a doctor and I don't know how many pharmacist's mates got in. After they got there, we were always having alerts. There were planes flying around.

We were still at our battle stations and didn't know for sure what they were.

Then it was kinda quiet and it was sort of a lull for a few minutes, and everybody was kinda talking and breathing a little easy—everybody was pretty well shook up from the night before. I remember I was just relieving another man on my gun on the phones. We took turns every once in a while so it would be easier. It was pretty hard on your ears and everything, and I took over one phone. I was putting them on while he was taking the other ones off.

And I said to him, "Are you ready?" And he didn't say anything, he just looked at me, kinda with his mouth open. I didn't know what it was, somebody was passing the word over the phone or what. It just seemed like everybody was just standing there and then an explosion. A torpedo struck or something. It struck about midship because the whole thing just blew up and it threw me against a gun mount. I had one of these steel helmets on and when I came to, everything was all torn apart and there was oil coming down the air and I thought it was rain, but it was just the oil from the feed tanks or something. The tanks had blew up in the air.

And there was smoke and there was fellows laying all around there and parts of their gun shields torn apart and the fantail where I was

sticking almost straight up in the air. It was so slippery that you couldn't walk up it, and the guys that was still able to climb over the side couldn't walk up. They were crawling over the side and holding on the life line trying to pull themselves further aft and jump over. And they were jumping over and bumping into each other.

It was still so smoky and all, you couldn't quite see, and I was still hazy and I knew I had to get up and get off of there. I was afraid the suction would pull me down. When I went to get up, I felt this pain in my foot and I couldn't get my foot loose from the shield or something; it fell down on top of my right foot across the instep of it and I couldn't get loose. It was only a few seconds, and the water was closing in around the ship and there was just this little bit of it left. And I knew that I had to get off but I couldn't, and there was a lot of kapok life jackets laying around deck.

I grabbed one of them in my arms and held it. I didn't even put it on, and the water closed in around the ship and we went down. And I gave up; I just thought that there wasn't a chance at all—everything just run through my head. And you could see all objects in the water, all the fellows and everything, and after we were under the surface—I don't know how far, but the sheet of iron or whatever it

The night cruiser action of November 13, 1942, began with the Japanese sending a force to bombard Guadalcanal. An American force under Admiral Daniel J. Callaghan in the San Francisco *(above, left) intercepted. The Japanese were turned back, but Admiral Callaghan was killed, and the* Juneau *and one other ship, the* Atlanta, *were sunk.*

was, it was released and my foot came loose and then the buoyancy from the life jacket brought me back to the surface.

It was like a big whirlpool. There was oil very thick on the water, it was at least two inches thick—seemed that way, anyway—and there was all kinds of blueprints and drawings of the ship floating around. And then there was roll after roll of tissue paper, and that's about all there was on top. I couldn't see anybody. I thought, gee, am I the only one here? My head was very hazy and I didn't think a thing about the other ships. I put the life jacket on when I came to the top, and I paddled around the water.

I don't know how long—it wasn't too long —when this doughnut life raft just popped right up in front of me. I don't know where it came from; it just seemed to come up there. I grabbed it and held on, and then I heard a man cry. I looked around and it was this boatswain's mate second class. His name—I can't quite remember his name. If I could see it, I'd recognize it. He was in the post office on the ship and he was crying for help. I went over to help him.

He said he couldn't swim and he had his whole leg torn off, blew off. I helped him on the doughnut raft and then gradually one by one some more stragglers would come and we'd all get on.

Everybody was kinda scared at first. Some of them couldn't swim; they were afraid they'd lose their grip and drown. So it went on that way and then these B-17 Flying Fortresses flew over the area. They just skimmed the water and they'd wave to us.*

Well, by nightfall we were about three doughnuts together. [The doughnut is a large circular float supporting a rope net, accommodating a good many partially submerged men.] It just lays on the water and you try to lay on top of it. Well, there was a lot of fellows on them. I should say there was about 140 of us when we all got together. Some of them were in very bad shape. Their arms and legs were torn off. And one of them, I could see myself his skull. You could see the red part inside where his head had been split open. They were all crying together and very down in the dumps and wondering if anybody was ever going to pick them up. And they thought, well, at least tomorrow there will be somebody out here. And that night—it was a very hard night because the fellows who were wounded badly were all in agony. And in the morning this fellow that had his head torn open, his hair had turned gray just like he was an old man. It turned gray right overnight.

The oil was so thick it sort of made everybody sick to their stomachs. So we decided to try to get out of the oil. Where the water was clear it didn't bother you so much, but then we worried because we knew there were sharks in those waters.

Then Lieutenant Blodgett—he was gunnery officer, he was a full lieutenant on the *Juneau*—he took charge of the party and he decided that we ought to try to paddle for land because we could see land when we first went down. And what we done, we secured the doughnuts together, one behind another in a line and the fellows that were able would get up in the forward ones and straddle legs over it [the floats] and paddle. And we done that all day. We took turns. All that night we done the same thing. And the lieutenant was supposed to be navigating by the stars.

Well, we didn't seem to be getting anywhere at all because the doughnuts were so clumsy. The ones who were wounded that hadn't died already had narrowed down to about 50 men. The ones of us who were in the best shape, we tried to swim around and help out the other ones. And some of the fellows—there was some planks there—they decided they'd try to swim for land on these planks. Well, they tried to do it and I never did see a couple of them again, but this one fellow came back; he found out he couldn't make it and he came back to our party on this big wooden plank.

Well, the sea began to get rough again. In the daytime the sun was very hot and I found out that the fellows who took their shirts off, or the ones that had them torn off by the explosion, their backs, their skin had all burned. And the ones of us who kept our clothes on were in the best shape because of the oil in the clothes. That protected us. At night it was very cold; you'd have to keep under the water to keep yourself warm. In the daytime the oil in the clothes would keep the sun off you, wouldn't penetrate your body so much.

But then on the fourth day the sea was very rough; the doughnuts began to separate. There were about 12 on mine. There was a gunner's mate second, his name was—it's so long ago, I'm forgetting the names of all these fellows— well anyway, there was him, there was a boat-

According to Morison's book on the Guadalcanal battles, the *Helena*, whose captain was now senior officer present, asked a Flying Fortress to notify the South Pacific command that *Juneau* had been torpedoed and that survivors were in the water, but this message did not get through. Admiral William F. Halsey, Jr., later relieved the captain of his command for abandoning the survivors. It can be argued that it was too hazardous to stop in these waters then, especially for wounded ships, but lifeboats and rafts could have been dropped.

COMBAT ART SECTION, U.S. NAVY

swain's mate and myself and this George Sullivan, he was gunner's mate second. I think he was the oldest brother of the Sullivans, he was on the raft with me. There was several others; there was a Polish fellow from somewhere in Pennsylvania. I remember him talking about he was a coal miner before the war. And then there was a fellow from Tennessee.

We tried to paddle and we found it wasn't doing no good so we decided just to lay there and hope that someone would find us.

Airplanes did fly over and some of them would come down close to us and some of them wouldn't, and after a while some of the fellows were getting very delirious and, if a few waved at a plane that went by, they'd get mad at you, say you were crazy for doing it, and not to pay any attention to the planes. They didn't want to save us and they were going to leave us there. Well, I always thought that probably there was still battles going on and they couldn't send a ship out there and if we just hung on, sometime somebody would come and get us.

They knew we were there, I knew that, so when they could send a ship, they'd come. Some of the guys was kinda disappointed and

pretty low in mind, so they sorta gave up. There's one fellow, he was a gunner's mate from the *Juneau,* second class. Well, he kept swallowing salt water all the time and he'd let his head fall down in the water and swallow it and he'd begin to get very dopey and dreary. He couldn't help himself at all, so I held him up. I held him in my arms, his head above the water as much as I could, and I held him that way all afternoon. Towards night he got stiff and I told the other fellows.

I said, "Well, how about holding him a while? I can't hold him, I've got all to do to hold myself." And they said they wouldn't do it, they were arguing and fighting among themselves a lot. And I said, "I felt his heart and his wrists and I couldn't feel any beating." I figured he was dead and I said to them, "Well, I'm going to let him go."

And George Sullivan, the oldest brother of the Sullivans, he said to me, "You can't do that," he said. "It's against all regulations of the navy. You can't bury a man at sea without having official orders from some captain or the Navy Department or something like that." And I knew he was delirious and there was something wrong with him and all, but the

In this drawing of a rescue operation, a destroyer picks up men adrift in doughnut life rafts similar to the one in which Heyn floated for nine days.

other fellows, they wouldn't let me let him go.

I said to them, "Well, you hold him," and they wouldn't hold him. So it went on that way for a little while. His legs were hanging down in the water a little way below mine when a shark bit his leg, bit his leg right off below the knee. He didn't move or say anything. That was enough for me. I figured, well, I'm going to drop him. There isn't any sense holding a dead man. So we took his dog tag off, this one fellow did, and said a prayer for him and let him float away.

At night it was so cold for the fellows who didn't have no clothes, we'd try to huddle them among us to keep them warm under the water. The sharks kept getting worse in the daytime, and you could see them around us all the time. We'd kick them with our feet and splash the water and they'd keep away. But at night you'd get drowsy and you'd kinda fall asleep and you wouldn't see them coming. As night went on, they'd come and they'd grab a guy every once in a while and bite him. And once they did, they wouldn't eat him altogether, they'd just take a piece of him and go away and then they'd come back and get him and drag him away and drown him. He'd scream and holler and everything, but there wasn't anything we could do.

And then the fellows got kind of ideas that the ship was sunk under us, sitting on the bottom. You could swim down there at night and get something to eat and all them kinda things, and I was beginning to believe them. Then one night they said we were carrying ammunition from one of the forward mounts back aft and, I don't know, they said they could see a light down there and this one fellow kept saying, "If it's down there, what are we staying up here for, let's go down there and get something to eat then." So I said, "You show me the way down there." So he dives under water and I went after him and I never did find nothing down there, no hatch or anything like he said was there. And then I got my sense again and I knew what I was doing and I didn't believe him any more.

The fifth day was coming up then. Things were getting pretty bad. The guys were fighting among themselves. If you bumped into one of them, he'd get mad and holler at you. And they did talk a lot about home and what they were going to do, and a lot of them said if they could get on an island, they'd stay there, they'd never go back to the navy. They didn't want to see it no more.

Well, this day the water was calm, and it was very hot. And the fellows that didn't have shirts on, the sun burned them something awful. It burned their skin all out, and their back, it was just like as if you shaved them with a razor or something, all raw and some of them just decided, they weren't going to try any more. They said they'd rather drown themselves than suffer like that. So that night after dark George Sullivan said he was going to take a bath. And he took off all his clothes and got away from the doughnut a little way and the white of his body must have flashed and showed up more because a shark came and grabbed him and that was the end of him. I never seen him again.

Towards morning, it was rough again and the waves were high and heavy. We were getting very hungry and it started drizzling rain. A sea gull flew around and it landed on our doughnut. We grabbed at him and we missed. Then he come back and that time we caught him and wrung his neck. There was about three or four of us, I don't remember for sure, and we ate the sea gull. There wasn't much of it.

Well, another night went on and the next day, this gunner's mate second, his name was Stewart, he said that there was a hospital ship there and we were going to go over to it. There was three of us—him, me and another fellow —and he said that we should swim over to it and leave the doughnut. We didn't know whether to or not. You hated to leave it there because you knew if you got out in the water, you were gone. So he dove in the water and swam off and he just kept swimming out over the water and he wouldn't turn around. You could see the sharks going after him and he swam and kicked and swam. And he hollered to us to come and get him with the raft, to paddle towards him but he kept swimming the other way. We paddled towards him and

The five Sullivan brothers—Joseph, Francis, Albert, Madison, and George—were all lost when the Juneau *went down. A destroyer was later named after them.*

finally he got tired. He turned around and came towards us and he got back before the sharks got him.

But that night it got cold again. He had thrown all his clothes away and he didn't have a thing and he wanted me to give him my clothes. But I said no, there's no sense to that. And he said, "Well, then I'm going down to the ship and get a clean suit. I got a lot of them in my locker." He also said, "I got a case of peaches in my gun mount."

He was really thinking the ship was down there. I wouldn't let him go because I knew if he dove down into the water something would happen to him. So I kept talking him out of it. And I kept him in between us to keep him warm. Well, that night he decided he wouldn't stand it no more. He just swam away and the sharks got him.

Well, then there was just the two of us left. And it was about the seventh day or so. We talked a lot that day together and I remember I gave my knife to this Mexican boy. He was trying to secure the raft again on his end. We were at each end with our feet kinda up in the water so we could fight the sharks off better. That night we got kinda sleepy and we dozed off I guess, because a shark grabbed him and tore his leg off below, just jaggedy like. And

he complained, he said to me that somebody was stabbing him with a knife. I said, "How can anybody stab you out here? There's nobody but us two."

And he swore at me and called me all kinds of names and said I had to get him to a doctor. I guess I was delirious, because I was paddling and paddling in the water there. I didn't know where I was going. I was just paddling, trying to get him to a doctor. Well, finally he screamed and hollered and he came over to me and I held his arm and then I could see what it was. I knew that he had been bit by a shark and I held him and the shark came up and it just grabbed him underneath and kept eating him from the bottom and pulling on him. Well, I couldn't hold him any more. The sharks just pulled him down under the water and he drowned. Well then, that's all that happened. It seemed like the night would never end.

The next day I just floated around some more, and it went on like that for the next couple of days and in the morning of the last day, which was the ninth day, I began to get delirious myself. I see these guys come up out of the water. It looked like to me that they had rifles on their backs and I'd holler to them

1347

and they said they were up there on guard duty. They'd come up from each hatch on the ship. Well, I asked them how it was. And they said the ship was all right, you could go down there and get something dry and eat. So I said to them, well, I'll come over there by you and go down with you. Well, I swam over to them and they just disappeared. I went back. I done that twice. Each time they disappeared when I got there. And then my head got clear and something told me just to hang on a little longer.

And about noontime that day a PBY [Catalina seaplane] flew over and circled around and then it went away again. Well, I gave up. I figured, well, I guess it's just like all the other planes, they ain't gonna bother; they figure you ain't worth while coming for. Or maybe they didn't know what I was because I was all black. I might have been a Jap for all they knew. A couple of hours later they come back and they flew around me and they dropped smoke bombs all around me.

Well, that built up my hope a lot and I took off my shirt and I waved at them and they waved back at me and then they went off and I could see them way off flying. And I figured, well, they must be guiding the ship to me. And that's what they were doing because it wasn't long before I could see the mast of a ship coming over the horizon and it was the U.S.S. *Ballard* [a destroyer]. They lowered a small boat and came out and picked me up and that's about all, for I went on there into sick bay.

[Heyn recalls that he was rescued on November 22, 1942. He was delirious when he was taken aboard the *Ballard*, suffering from shock, exhaustion, and a broken foot. Eventually he was brought to Fiji, where he spent nine months in a naval hospital.]

LT. PORTER: Think you're fully recovered?

HEYN: I think I'm all right.

LT. PORTER: Good. Having fully recovered, you then asked for and were given submarine service. Is that right?

HEYN: Yes, that's right.

LT. PORTER: And you went out on a war patrol?

HEYN: Yes, sir.

LT. PORTER: And on that patrol, you're officially credited with sinking some five ships and damaging four?

HEYN: That's correct.

LT. PORTER: Your preference for future service would be in submarines?

HEYN: Yes, sir, it would.

LT. PORTER: Back in the same hunting area?

HEYN: It wouldn't make any difference as long as it's out in the Pacific somewhere.

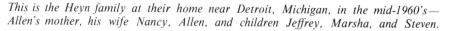

This is the Heyn family at their home near Detroit, Michigan, in the mid-1960's— Allen's mother, his wife Nancy, Allen, and children Jeffrey, Marsha, and Steven.

Volume 15

ENCYCLOPEDIC
SECTION

The two-page reference guide below lists the entries by categories. The entries in this section supplement the subject matter covered in the text of this volume. A **cross-reference** (*see*) means that a separate entry appears elsewhere in this section. However, certain important persons and events mentioned here have individual entries in the Encyclopedic Section of another volume. Consult the Index in Volume 18.

AMERICAN STATESMEN AND POLITICIANS

Theodore G. Bilbo
James F. Byrnes
Dwight D. Eisenhower
Harry Hopkins
Cordell Hull
Robert H. Jackson
George C. Marshall

Henry Morgenthau, Jr.
Franklin D. Roosevelt
Walter Bedell Smith
Edward R. Stettinius, Jr.
Harry S. Truman
James W. Wadsworth, Jr.
Sumner Welles
Wendell Willkie

THE ATOMIC AGE

Atomic Bomb
Albert Einstein

Manhattan Project
Harold C. Urey

FOREIGN RELATIONS

Atlantic Charter
Cairo Conference
Casablanca Conference
Iron Curtain

Nuremberg Trials
Potsdam Conference
Teheran Conference
Yalta Conference

FOREIGN STATESMEN AND POLITICIANS

Clement R. Atlee
Neville Chamberlain
Chiang Kai-Shek
Sir Winston Churchill

Francisco Franco
Adolf Hitler
Benito Mussolini
Joseph Stalin
Hideki Tojo

THOUGHT AND CULTURE

W. E. B. Du Bois
Albert Einstein

Eugene O'Neill
Asa P. Randolph
Thomas J. Watson

WORLD WAR II

Omar Bradley
Mark Clark
James Doolittle
Dwight D. Eisenhower
Frank J. Fletcher
William F. Halsey
Thomas Kinkaid
William D. Leahy
Douglas MacArthur
George C. Marshall

Bernard L. Montgomery
Chester W. Nimitz
George S. Patton, Jr.
Matthew B. Ridgway
Erwin Rommel
Walter Bedell Smith
Raymond A. Spruance
Joseph W. Stilwell
Jonathan M. Wainwright
Isoroku Yamamoto

A

ATLANTIC CHARTER. This charter was a joint statement of principles and general postwar aims issued by President **Franklin D. Roosevelt** and Prime Minister **Winston Churchill** (*see both*) on August 14, 1941 (*see pp. 1271–1272*). It was drawn up by the two leaders with the aid of the American Undersecretary of State, **Sumner Welles** (*see*), and the British Undersecretary of State for Foreign Affairs, Sir Alexander Cadogan (1884–1968), during a series of secret meetings held alternately aboard the United States cruiser *Augusta* and the British battleship *Prince of Wales* off the coast of Newfoundland August 9–12, 1941. Although not an official document —that is, it was never submitted for ratification, for example, to the United States Senate—both Roosevelt and Churchill signed it as a pledge of their joint cooperation. The Atlantic Charter contained eight points. The two leaders pledged themselves to (1) the renunciation of territorial or other aggrandizement; (2) the opposition to territorial changes contrary to the desires of the peoples concerned; (3) the support of the right of self-government and the restoration of sovereign rights and self-government to those forcibly deprived of them; (4) the furtherance of international economic prosperity by striving to give all nations equal access to trade and raw materials; (5) the establishment of international collaboration to secure improved economic and social conditions for all; (6) the establishment of a peace that would afford all men freedom from fear and want; (7) the establishment of freedom of the seas; (8) the abandonment of the use of force and the disarmament of aggressor nations

Churchill planned the divine service that opened the Atlantic Charter talks.

pending the establishment of a permanent peace-keeping structure. These principles were subsequently incorporated into the charter of the United Nations (*see pp. 1311–1331*).

ATOMIC BOMB. *See* **Manhattan Project.**

ATTLEE, Clement Richard (1883–1967). The leader of Britain's Labor Party for 20 years, Attlee became prime minister in 1945 when the Conservative Party under the leadership of **Winston Churchill** (*see*) was voted out of office. The Labor Party's landslide victory that year was the result of a widespread desire for immediate social reforms. As prime minister (1945–1951), Attlee transformed Britain into a welfare state, nationalizing many of its most important industries. He also led the movement that culminated in the independence of India, Ceylon, Burma, Pakistan, and Palestine. Born in London, Attlee was educated at Oxford and was admitted to the bar in 1905. His interest in law was soon overshadowed by his concern for reforms, and from 1907 to 1914 he devoted himself to social work in London's poverty-stricken East End. During this period, Attlee became a Socialist, taught social science at the

London School of Economics, and was active in organizing the modern Labor Party. In 1914, he volunteered for service in World War I and subsequently saw action in the Mideast and France, emerging with the rank of major. By the time Attlee entered Parliament in 1922, he was well-known in Labor circles. He entered the cabinet of Labor Prime Minister Ramsay MacDonald (1866–1937) in 1930 but resigned the following year when MacDonald formed a coalition government. During the next four years, Attlee opposed pacifism and advocated strong British resistance to the totalitarian regimes of **Adolf Hitler** and **Benito Mussolini** (*see both*). After he became leader of the Labor Party in the House of Commons in 1935, he led his party's attack on the Conservatives for their policy of nonintervention in the Spanish Civil War (1936–1939). He also opposed the appeasement policy of Prime Minister **Neville Chamberlain** (*see*) toward Germany and Italy. In May, 1940, Attlee entered Churchill's wartime coalition government as Lord Privy Seal. He held several other important cabinet posts and ultimately became deputy prime minister. In this last capacity he headed the government when Churchill was away or indisposed. During his six years as prime minister, Attlee cooperated closely with the United States on matters of foreign policy. He supported America in its cold war with the Soviet Union but advised President **Harry S. Truman** (*see*) to fight a limited war in Korea. After Churchill and his Conservative Party were voted back into power in 1951, Attlee served as the leader of the opposition until his retirement in 1955. That year, he received an earldom. He published his autobiography, *As It Happened,* in 1954 and his memoirs, *Twilight of Empire,* in 1962.

B

BILBO, Theodore Gilmore (1877–1947). A Democratic Senator from Mississippi whose name became synonymous with demagoguery, bigotry, and political corruption, Bilbo was denied his seat in the 80th Congress for allegedly taking bribes from defense contractors during World War II and for conspiring to deprive black citizens of their rights during his victorious campaign for reelection in 1946. A native of Poplarville, Mississippi. Bilbo received his Baptist lay preacher's license while still in his teens. After attending Peabody College in Nashville, Tennessee, he studied law at Vanderbilt University. Bilbo was admitted to the bar in 1908, the same year he won election to a four-year term in the Mississippi senate. From 1912 to 1916, he was lieutenant governor of Mississippi, and he twice served (1916–1920 and 1928–1932) as governor. Despite frequent accusations of dishonesty, Bilbo was repeatedly supported by his back-country constituents, who applauded his bombastic and white-supremacist oratory. As governor, Bilbo sought to change the Mississippi educational system to his liking, firing faculty members and appointing a public-relations man as president of a college. Bilbo also secured passage of a multimillion-dollar highway bond issue that left the state on the verge of bankruptcy. Between his terms as governor, he found employment with the Agricultural Adjustment Administration in Washington, D. C., where, asked to snip clippings from newspapers, he billed himself as the "Pastemaster General." Elected to the first of two terms (1935–1947) in the Senate in 1934, Bilbo won notoriety for his support of poll taxes, his opposition to the Fair Employment Practices Act, and his efforts to deport blacks to Africa. Shortly before the Democratic primary in Mississippi in 1946, Bilbo, a member of the Ku Klux Klan, said, "I'm calling on every red-blooded American who believes in the superiority and integrity of the white race to get out and see that no nigger votes. And the best time to do it is the night before." Suffering from cancer and heart disease, Bilbo died in 1947 before the matter of his seating in Congress could be resolved. His book,

Theodore G. Bilbo

Take Your Choice—Segregation or Mongrelization, was published in 1947.

BRADLEY, Omar Nelson (1893–1981). Bradley commanded the First United States Army in the Normandy invasion on D-Day, June 6, 1944 (*see pp. 1275–1289*). and during the subsequent Allied liberation of France from German control. He then assumed command of the 1,300,000-man Twelfth Army Group—the most massive American combat unit ever assembled—which, by the spring of 1945, had smashed Axis resistance in the battle for Germany. Between 1949 and 1953, Bradley served as the first permanent chairman of the Joint Chiefs of Staff, the highest military office in the armed services. A native of Missouri, Bradley graduated from West Point in 1915. After attaining the temporary rank of major while serving with the Fourteenth Infantry Regiment during World War I, he held numerous military teaching and administrative assignments over the next 20 years. During the 1920s, he taught mathematics at West Point and administered national guard and reserve units in Hawaii. Throughout the following decade, he was an instructor at the Fort Benning (Georgia) Infantry School and at West Point and was assigned to staff duty in Washington, D. C. Promoted from lieutenant colonel to brigadier general in 1941, Bradley served as commandant of the infantry school in Georgia until 1942, when he was raised to major general and made a divisional commander. Early in 1943, General **Dwight D. Eisenhower** (*see*) sent Bradley to North Africa as his personal representative. Placed in charge of the American II Corps, Bradley led that unit in campaigns in Tunisia and Sicily that cleared the path

Omar Bradley

for the Allied invasion of Italy. He then assumed leadership of the First Army, which played a central role in the successful Normandy campaign. After the war, Bradley served as administrator of veterans' affairs from 1945 until 1948, when he succeeded General Eisenhower as the Army Chief of Staff. From 1949 until his retirement four years later, he occupied the newly created post of chairman of the Joint Chiefs. He was promoted to the five-star rank of General of the Army in 1950 and the following year published his autobiography, *A Soldier's Story*. Bradley entered business after his retirement.

BYRNES, James Francis (1879–1972). In nearly a half-century of public service, this South Carolina Democrat held important posts in every branch of the government—legislative, executive, and judicial. Born in Charleston, South Carolina, Byrnes quit school at the age of 14 to help support his family. He taught himself law and was admitted to the bar in 1903. Byrnes soon became active in local politics and beginning in

1910 was elected to seven consecutive terms (1911–1925) in the House of Representatives. In 1930, he was elected to the first of two Senate terms (1931–1941). At first a liberal, Byrnes was instrumental in pushing much of the New Deal legislation of **Franklin D. Roosevelt** (*see*) through the Senate. After 1936, however, his enthusiasm for the New Deal waned, although he maintained good relations with the President and assisted him in launching his defense program in 1940. The following year, Byrnes was named to fill a vacancy on the Supreme Court. He served only a year as an Associate Justice, resigning in 1942 to become Director of Economic Stabilization. In 1943, Byrnes was chosen to head the newly created War Mobilization Board. In this capacity he exercised complete control over the production of military and civilian goods and stabilized the wartime economy. He also accompanied Roosevelt to the **Yalta Conference** (*see*) in February, 1945. Byrnes subsequently succeeded **Edward R. Stettinius, Jr.** (*see*) as Secretary of State. He attended the **Potsdam Conference** with President **Harry S. Truman** (*see both*) and negotiated with world leaders at other meetings in London and Moscow. In September, 1946, at the 21-nation Paris Peace Conference, he insisted that a healthy Germany was essential to a reconstructed Europe. Byrnes resigned from the State Department in 1947. Reentering state politics, he became a major spokesman for conservative Southern Democrats, and in 1950 was elected governor (1951–1955) of South Carolina. As such, he upheld states' rights and denounced Truman's spending programs and the "socialistic experimentation of the welfare state." In 1952, he supported Republican **Dwight D.**

Eisenhower (*see*) for President. A conservative on racial issues, Byrnes, while governor, maintained segregation in South Carolina's public schools. He has written *Speaking Frankly* (1947) and the autobiographical *All in One Lifetime* (1958).

C

CAIRO CONFERENCE. Generalissimo **Chiang Kai-shek** of China, President **Franklin D. Roosevelt** of the United States, and Prime Minister **Winston Churchill** of Great Britain (*see all*) met together for the first time in Cairo, Egypt, November 22–26, 1943, to discuss war strategy in the Far East. Chiang Kai-shek and Roosevelt favored an amphibious operation in Burma, but Churchill resisted the plan. They finally decided to support troops in the area with air attacks. The conferees declared that Japan would "be expelled from all territories which she has taken by violence and greed," a declaration modified and extended in Russia's favor at the **Yalta Conference** (*see*). Manchuria, Formosa, and the Pescadores were to be restored to China, and Korea was to become free and independent "in due course." After Japan's defeat, however, Russia, according to the terms agreed upon at Yalta, occupied the area north of the 38th parallel in Korea, facing United States forces to the south. A Communist government was established in the north and a Western-oriented government in the south—a situation that led, in 1950, to the Korean War. Churchill and Roosevelt left Cairo to meet with Premier **Joseph Stalin** of Russia at the **Teheran Conference** (*see both*). Subsequently, Roosevelt and Churchill returned to Cairo to meet with the president of

Turkey, Ismet Inonu (born 1884). Although Turkey remained neutral, Inonu indicated his support of Allied plans.

CASABLANCA CONFERENCE.
Shortly after the successful Allied invasion of North Africa, the Casablanca Conference was held to formulate long-range plans for the prosecution of World War II and to coordinate the operation of the Free French forces. President **Franklin D. Roosevelt** of the United States and Prime Minister **Winston Churchill** of Great Britain (*see both*) met at the Hotel Anfa, four miles outside of Casablanca, French Morocco, from January 14 through January 24, 1943. Leaders of the rival Free French factions, General Charles de Gaulle (1890–1970) and General Henri Giraud (1879–1949), also attended some of the sessions. Premier **Joseph Stalin** of Russia and Generalissimo **Chiang Kai-shek** of China (*see both*) did not attend but were kept informed of developments. Although the British were reluctant to make long-range commitments, it was decided that Sicily and then Italy would be invaded from North Africa as soon as Tunisia was made secure. A final decision on the opening of a second front, the invasion of France, was delayed. Stalin was particularly displeased when he received this news and suspected the Allies of stalling. Admiral **Chester Nimitz** and General **Douglas MacArthur** (*see both*) were given permission to start an offensive against the Japanese in the Pacific, but priority was still given to the defeat of Germany. The Allies agreed to wage war until the enemy surrendered unconditionally, a position that was criticized by those who thought it stiffened the enemy's resistance. Following the Casablanca Conference, Churchill and

F. D. R. parlayed with Giraud, de Gaulle, and Churchill at Casablanca.

Roosevelt met again in Quebec, Canada, in August, 1943, to discuss the war against Japan. By the end of the summer, Russo-American relations were quite strained. In October, however, American Secretary of State **Cordell Hull** (*see*), British Foreign Minister Anthony Eden (1897–1977), and Russian Foreign Minister Vyacheslav Molotov (1890–1986) met in Moscow and worked out the procedures of Allied cooperation. Russia agreed at the Moscow Conference with the concept of a United Nations. The following month, Roosevelt, Churchill, and Stalin met for the first time at the **Teheran Conference** (*see*).

CHAMBERLAIN, Arthur Neville
(1869–1940). Neville Chamberlain, who served as prime minister of Britain from 1937 to 1940, was known for his policy of appeasement in the face of repeated aggression by Nazi Germany. The treaty he signed with **Adolf Hitler** (*see*)—the Munich Pact—has become synonymous with making concessions that will open the way to further intimidation and domination. Chamberlain enjoyed a successful career as a businessman in his native Birmingham, of which he was Lord Mayor (1915–1916) before entering Parliament as a Conservative in 1918. He held several cabinet positions over the next two decades before becoming prime minister. Hopeful of settling Germany's claims in the Sudetenland through negotiations, and remembering the loss of millions of British and French soldiers during World War I, Chamberlain sought to avoid war "because of a quarrel in a far-away country between people of whom we know nothing." He went to Munich in 1938 to meet with

representatives of France, Germany, and Italy. Under the terms of the Munich Pact, signed on September 30, 1938, France and Britain granted Germany the German-inhabited Sudetenland, an area of Czechoslovakia, in return for its pledge that the Nazi government would not insist on any other territorial concessions in Europe. Chamberlain came back from Munich claiming that he had made "peace in our time" (*see p. 1266*). However, many prominent statesmen, including **Winston Churchill** (*see*), opposed his appeasement policy and believed that Hitler would not keep his word. It was only after Hitler annexed Czech-speaking areas of Czechoslovakia the following March and invaded Poland in September, 1939, that Chamberlain reversed his policy and declared war on Germany. Widely criticized for having underestimated Hitler's aims, Chamberlain stepped down as prime minister in favor of Churchill in May, 1940, and assumed the less important cabinet post of Lord President of the Council. Ill health forced him to resign the following October.

CHIANG KAI-SHEK (1887–1975). Head of the Chinese Nationalist government and archenemy of communism, Generalissimo Chiang Kai-shek held his country together during the Japanese invasion (1937–1945), only to lose control of the mainland to the Communists in the early postwar years. A native of Chekiang Province on the east coast of China, Chiang attended Paoting Military Academy in China and graduated from the Tokyo Military Academy in 1909. For the next year, he served in the Japanese army. While in Japan, he met the founder of the Chinese Republic, Dr. Sun Yat-sen (1866–1925), and became his protégé. After

the Chinese Revolution of 1911, power fell into the hands of army officers who, armed with modern weapons, set themselves up as provincial warlords. Chiang supported Dr. Sun, who tried to set up a democratic republic at Canton. In 1923, Sun's Kuomintang (National People's Party) allied itself with the Soviet Union, which sent him arms and advisers led by Mikhail Borodin (1884–1953). Chiang was sent to Russia to study its political and military systems. Returning to Canton in 1924, he founded the Whampoa Military Academy and after Sun's death led a military expedition against the warlords (1926–1928). Fearful of the growing power of the Chinese Communist Party led by Mao-Tse-tung (1893–1976), Chiang massacred a Communist army at Shanghai, expelled the Russians, and allied himself with the rich merchants of the east coast. Later that year, he married Mei-ling Soong (born 1898), sister-in-law of the late Dr. Sun and the daughter of Shanghai's richest merchant. American-educated and a Methodist, she converted Chiang to Christianity and became his most trusted adviser. Chiang continued his northward advance, taking Peking in 1928 and becoming generalissimo of all Nationalist forces. However, his alliance with Chang Hsueh-liang (born 1898), warlord of Manchuria, so frightened the Japanese that they occupied that province and expelled Chang and his army. But Chiang Kai-shek continued to consolidate his regime and in 1934 completely expelled the remaining Communists from South China. Mao led his army to the barren hills of Shensi in the north. War continued between the Nationalists and the Communists until Chang Hsueh-liang kidnapped Chiang Kai-shek in December, 1936, and forced

him to ally with the Communists against the Japanese. Japan, fearful of this united front, invaded China eight months later. Chiang's armies were driven from all of northern and eastern China. Only the Communists, using guerrilla tactics, were successful against the Japanese. After 1940, the bulk of Chiang's troops were committed to fighting the Communists rather than the Japanese. When Japan attacked Britain and the United States in 1941, Chiang was named Supreme Commander of Allied air and ground forces in the Chinese war theater. As such, he attended the 1943 **Cairo Conference** with **Franklin D. Roosevelt** and **Winston Churchill** (*see all*). At home, however, Chiang's friends, cut off from their wealth by the Japanese conquest, profiteered in the supplies sent by the Western powers. Toward the end of World War II, Russia defeated Japanese forces in Manchuria. As a result, Mao's troops picked up huge stocks of Japanese weapons. The United States sent Chiang more than $2,000,000,000 in supplies and aid between 1945 and 1949, and **George C. Marshall** (*see*), then the American ambassador to China, tried but failed to bring the two sides together. Chiang was elected as the first constitutional president of China in 1948 but refused to allow Communists into his government. By October, 1949, the Communists had driven the Nationalists off the mainland to exile on the island of Formosa (Taiwan). Chaing Kai-shek continued to rule Taiwan as the Republic of China until 1972 when he turned the government over to his eldest son, Chiang Ching-kuo (born 1910). With U.S. recognition of the People's Republic of China as the sole, legal government of China in 1979, formal relations with the Taiwan government were discontinued.

CHURCHILL, Sir Winston Leonard Spencer (1874–1965). Britain's greatest statesman and one of the free world's most admired leaders, Churchill was twice prime minister (1940–1945 and 1951–1955) and led Britain to victory in World War II. Churchill, who was the son of Lord Randolph Henry Spencer Churchill (1849–1895) and his American-born wife, the former Jennie Jerome (1854–1921), graduated from Sandhurst—Britain's West Point. He served with the Indian army and took part in one of the world's last great cavalry charges at the Battle of Omdurman in the Sudan during Britain's successful campaign to reconquer the Sudan in 1898. He later covered the Boer War (1899–1900) in South Africa as a war correspondent, and after being captured and escaping, served as a lieutenant. Churchill's political career began in 1900 when he was elected to Parliament as a Conservative. Three years later, he bolted that party to join the Liberals and subsequently held several cabinet posts before serving as First Lord of the Admiralty (1911–1915). In this capacity, Churchill modernized and increased the navy so that it was well prepared when World War I began. He also backed the ill-fated Dardanelles campaign of March, 1915, in which a combined French and British fleet attemped to take the Dardanelles. The successful completion of this operation would have eliminated Turkey from the war and would have given the Allies access to the Black Sea and Russia. When the campaign failed, largely because of naval incompetence, Churchill was ousted from the Admiralty. He later saw action in France before resuming his seat in the House of Commons in the fall of 1916. He again held cabinet posts

before losing his seat in 1922. Reelected once again as a Conservative two years later, he served as chancellor of the exchequer from 1924 to 1929 but during most of the next decade remained in Parliament without holding a ministerial position. During this period, Churchill warned that the Nazi government of **Adolf Hitler** (*see*) was a threat to world peace and opposed the appeasement policy advocated by **Neville Chamberlain** (*see*). On September 3, 1939, two days after World War II broke out, Chamberlain appointed him First Lord of the Admiralty. The following May, he replaced Chamberlain as prime minister, assuming the additional post of minister of defense. Establishing a coalition government to press the war, Churchill declared, "I have nothing to offer but blood, toil, tears, and sweat." The tough, cigar-smoking Churchill became the symbol of Britain's determination to win the conflict, and his "V for victory" hand sign became the Allied symbol of hope. In 1941, he met with President **Franklin D. Roosevelt** at sea to formulate the **Atlantic Charter** (*see both*). After the United States and the Soviet Union entered the war on Britain's side, Churchill made several trips to Washington and Moscow to keep the alliance together. Churchill also attended many international conferences (*see* **Cairo, Casablanca, Potsdam, Teheran,** and **Yalta Conferences**). During the crucial Battle of Britain in the fall of 1940, he paid tribute to the Royal Air Force, saying, "Never in the field of human conflict was so much owed by so many to so few." In 1945, with victory near, the British people, impatient for rapid social reforms, voted Churchill out of office. He then became leader of the Opposition,

and in 1946, in a speech at Fulton, Missouri, Churchill predicted a new threat, that of the Soviet Union. Urging a close Anglo-American alliance, Churchill coined the expression "iron curtain" to refer to the invisible barrier that was growing between Russia and the West. Churchill was again chosen as prime minister in 1951, and two years later he was awarded the Nobel Prize for literature for his writing and his oratory. He resigned in 1955 because of age but remained in the House of Commons until, nearing 90 in 1964, he announced that he would not seek reelection. Churchill, who was a talented amateur landscape painter, also wrote numerous books, including a four-volume history of World War I, *World Crisis* (1923–1929), a six-volume history of *The Second World War* (1948–1953), and the four-volume *A History of the English-speaking Peoples* (1956–1958). In April, 1963, he was made the first honorary citizen of the United States by a special act of Congress.

CLARK, Mark Wayne (1896–1984). During World War II, this well-known American general commanded the Fifth Army in North Africa and Italy. A career officer born in upstate New York, Clark graduated from West Point in 1917. He rose through the ranks and in May, 1942, was appointed Chief of Staff of the Army Ground Forces. Two months later, he became commander of Army Ground Forces in the European Theater of Operations and in this capacity played a major role in planning the Allied invasion of French North Africa. In January, 1943, he was made commanding general of the Fifth Army, the first American army active in Europe. Headquartered in Oujda, North Africa, he spent the next seven months preparing his forces for the amphibious invasion of Italy that took place on September 9, 1943 (*see pp. 1297–1298*). He landed at Salerno, where he was met by heavy German defenses. Soon afterward, he joined forces with the British Eighth Army under

Mark Clark

Lieutenant General (later Field Marshal) **Bernard L. Montgomery** (*see*), and after a treacherous winter, the Allies captured and liberated Rome on June 4, 1944. The following December, Clark was made commander of the Fifteenth Army Group, which comprised all the Allied fighting forces in Italy and was composed of the American Fifth and the British Eighth Armies. Promoted to the rank of full general in March, 1945, Clark was responsible for launching the drive that led to the unconditional surrender of German forces in Italy, several Austrian provinces, and sections of Carinthia and Styria on May 2, 1945, four days before the termination of hostilities in Western Europe. He subsequently served (1945–1947) as commander of the United States occupation force in Austria and as United States High Commis-

sioner for Austria. After military service in the United States (1947–1952), he was appointed head of United Nations forces in Korea and of the United States Far East Command. On July 27, 1953, he signed the Korean truce agreement that ended the Korean War, and the following October he retired from the army. In 1953, Clark became president of The Citadel, The Military College of South Carolina, which is situated in Charleston. He has written *Calculated Risk* (1950) and *From the Danube to the Yalu* (1954), his memoirs of World War II and the Korean War, respectively.

D

DOOLITTLE, James (born 1896). "Jimmy" Doolittle was the Army Air Force officer who planned and led the first American bombing raid over Japan during World War II. The aviator began his military career in 1917, enlisting in the army as a flying cadet. After being trained as a pilot, he served as a flight and gunnery instructor. Following the war, Doolittle remained in the service, where he established a reputation as a high-speed test pilot. In 1922, he became the first man to fly across America in less than one day. With only one stop, he covered the distance from Pablo Beach, Florida, to San Diego, California, in 21 hours, 19 minutes. In 1929, Doolittle became the first pilot to fly "blind," using horizontal and directional gyroscopes that he helped develop to navigate. Retiring from the army the next year, he became manager of the aviation department of the Shell Oil Company (1930–1940). Doolittle was recalled to active duty as a lieutenant colonel in 1940. Two years later, he won worldwide fame when he led 16

medium bombers on the first air raid over Japan. The specially trained crews took off from the carrier *Hornet* while 670 miles from Japan and struck Tokyo on April 18, 1942. Although the bombs did little damage, the raid, made after a series of American setbacks in the Pacific, was a boost to American morale. Of the 16 planes, only one fell into Japanese territory. One plane landed in Russian Siberia and its crew was detained for 13 months. The remaining 14 planes, including Doolittle's, landed in Nationalist China. Doolittle, who subsequently flew to India over the Himalayas, was promoted to brigadier general and given the Medal of Honor on his return home to the United States. That same year, he was made commander in chief of the 12th Air Force in North Africa. In 1943, he headed the 15th Air Force in the Mediterranean Theater and the following year commanded the Eighth Air Force in Europe on D-Day, June 6, 1944 (*see pp. 1275–1289*), before returning to the Pacific. Doolittle left the army in 1946, returning to the Shell Oil Company as a vice-president.

DU BOIS, William Edward Burghardt (1868–1963). Writing early in his career that "The problem of the twentieth century is the problem of the color-line," this black historian and sociologist was a founder of the National Association for the Advancement of Colored People (NAACP) who sought to end racial discrimination in all phases of American life. Born in Great Barrington, Massachusetts, W. E. B. Du Bois attended Fisk University and earned his bachelor's degree from Harvard in 1890. Five years later, he became the first black to receive a doctorate from Harvard, and

W. E. B. Du Bois

afterward he taught history and economics at Atlanta University. In 1903, Du Bois challenged what he believed to be the subservient attitude of black leaders such as Booker T. Washington (1856–1915) toward whites in his first book, *The Souls of Black Folk.* Charging that Washington "practically accepts the alleged inferiority of the Negro races," Du Bois outlined a complete civil-rights program as an alternative. He maintained that each race had a "talented tenth" —that is, one person out of every 10 who had the ability to succeed —and that this was just as true of blacks as of any others. An activist, Du Bois in 1905 organized the Niagara Movement to work for black equality. Four years later, on the 100th anniversary of the birth of Abraham Lincoln (1809–1865), he organized, with the aid of both black and white reformers, the NAACP. As its director of research and publications, Du Bois started and edited the organization's magazine, *Crisis.* During a period of antiradical sentiment in 1919, *Crisis* fell under the scrutiny of the Justice Department. When asked the purpose of his journal. Du Bois replied that it was to uphold the Constitution and all its Amend-

ments. After 1932, Du Bois left his post with the NAACP and returned to Atlanta University, where he was a professor of sociology until 1944. Becoming more and more radical in outlook, Du Bois made a complete break with the NAACP in 1948 because of its nonmilitant approach in the civil-rights struggle. Much honored in his later years, Du Bois was chairman of the Peace Information Bureau in 1950–1951 and was awarded the Lenin International Peace Prize by the Soviet Union in 1958. That same year, he became the first black to be elected to the National Institute of Arts and Letters. Although he had long scorned the tactics of communism, Du Bois joined the Communist Party at the age of 93, and disillusioned with the lot of the American black intellectual, moved the following year to the African republic of Ghana, where he spent the remainder of his life compiling an unfinished *Encyclopedia Africana.* Among his books are two sociological studies, *John Brown* (1909) and *Black Reconstruction* (1935), and the autobiographical *Dusk of Dawn* (1940). The W. E. B. Du Bois Club, a nationwide left-wing organization that was started by Communists, was founded after his death.

E

EINSTEIN, Albert (1879–1955). A brilliant German-born physicist, Einstein conceived the theory of relativity, which paved the way for the understanding of atomic energy. As a boy, Einstein went to school in Munich, but he intentionally did not do well in school because he wanted to be with his family, which was then living in Milan, Italy. He left school when he was 16, and once in Milan he taught himself

calculus and higher mathematics in six months. In 1896, he entered the Polytechnic Academy at Zurich, Switzerland, graduating in 1900. Two years later, he began work as a patent examiner (1902–1909) at the Swiss patent office in Berne, while working for his Ph.D. at the University of Zurich. In 1905, Einstein published papers dealing with the photoelectric effect, the Brownian movement—that is, the motion of atoms—and his special theory of relativity—which postulated that $E = MC^2$, or Energy equals Mass multiplied by the Speed of Light squared. In 1916, he expanded his theory into the general theory of relativity. Einstein was awarded the Nobel Prize in 1921 for his work on the photoelectric effect. From 1914 to 1933, he was the director of the Kaiser Wilhelm Institute of Theoretical Physics

PHYSICS TODAY

Albert Einstein

in Berlin. With the rise of **Adolf Hitler** (*see*) in Germany, Einstein determined to immigrate to the United States. In 1933, he accepted a post at the Institute for Advanced Study at Princeton, New Jersey, where he remained until his death. The next year, 1934, the Nazi government revoked his citizenship and confiscated his property. Einstein's work in America was largely devoted to his unified-field theory, published in 1953. In this theory, he attempted to combine the laws of gravitation and electromagnetism. In 1939, Einstein wrote President **Franklin D. Roosevelt** (*see*), advising him of the possibility that German scientists had begun research that could result in atomic weapons. He urged the President to support nuclear research in America. This led to the establishment of the so-called **Manhattan Project** (*see*), in which a number of eminent physicists were able to develop the first atomic bomb in 1945. Einstein, who had become an American citizen in 1940, was a devoted pacifist and for several years after World War II was a leading figure in the movement for a single world government. In 1952, he turned down the opportunity to become the president of Israel. Einstein's last public statement was an appeal to end the nuclear-arms race. His nonscientific published works include *Why War?*, written with Sigmund Freud (1856–1939) in 1933, *The World As I See It* (1934), and *Out of My Later Years* (1950).

EISENHOWER, Dwight David (1890–1969). As Supreme Commander of the victorious Allied forces during World War II, Eisenhower achieved fame for his ability to lead one of the most successful combat coalitions in history (*see p. 1301*). This same talent for leadership was to play a large role in his later years as the 34th President of the United States. Eisenhower was a decendant of a family of German immigrants who came to America in 1732 and helped establish a Mennonite community in Penn-

sylvania. He was born in Denison, Texas, where his father, a resident of Kansas, was then employed. The family moved to Abilene, Kansas, in 1892, and there Dwight spent his boyhood. His schoolmates gave him the nickname Ike. After graduating from high school in 1909, Ike worked at various jobs in Abilene and played semiprofessional baseball. Although his father could not afford to send him to college, Ike won an appointment to West Point. He graduated 61st out of a class of 164 in 1915. While assigned as a second lieutenant to Fort Sam Houston in San Antonio, Texas, he met Mamie Geneva Doud (1896–1979) of Denver. The couple were wed on July 1, 1916. During World War I, Eisenhower taught at various army training centers in the United States and was promoted to major in 1920. In 1925, Eisenhower attended the army's Command and General Staff School at Fort Leavenworth. After graduating first in a class of 275 officers, he served at Fort Benning, Georgia. In 1927, he attended the army's War and Industrial Colleges. While later serving (1929–1933) under the Assistant Secretary of War, Eisenhower impressed General **Douglas MacArthur** (*see*), then the Army Chief of Staff. As MacArthur's assistant, Eisenhower went on an American military mission to Manila in 1935. He remained in the Philippines until the outbreak of World War II in Europe in 1939, when he returned to the United States and became an infantry officer. On December 14, 1941, seven days after the Japanese attacked Pearl Harbor, Eisenhower was called to Washington, D.C., by General **George C. Marshall** (*see*), the Army Chief of Staff. Marshall appointed him chief of operations and sent him to London in the spring of 1942

to study the organization and development of American forces in the European Theater of Operations (E.T.O.). Eisenhower was subsequently named commanding general of American forces in the E.T.O. by Marshall and began planning his first military campaign—the invasion of French North Africa, which was launched on November 8, 1942. That same day, Eisenhower was named the commander of all Allied forces in North Africa. Although his troops suffered a number of reverses at first and he was criticized for negotiating with French officials who had collaborated with the pro-Nazi Vichy regime, North Africa was liberated in May, 1943. Eisenhower next directed the conquest of Sicily that July. In September, he launched the invasion of Italy. His armies were unable to drive the Germans out of that country but did render the Italians powerless. In December, 1943, President **Franklin D. Roosevelt** (*see*) appointed Eisenhower, then a major general, Supreme Allied Commander of the Allied Expeditionary Force (A.E.F.) for the invasion of Europe. For nearly six months, Eisenhower planned the long-awaited second front. On June 6, 1944, the greatest invasion in history was launched across the English Channel (*see pp. 1275–1289*). Two months later, Eisenhower directed the invasion of southern France. By September, 1944, the Allies had reached the borders of Germany. When the Germans started their last major offensive of the war that December, called the Battle of the Bulge, he named British Field Marshal **Bernard L. Montgomery** (*see*) temporary commander of all troops north of the Bulge, including American forces under the command of General **Omar Bradley** (*see*). The Germans were eventually repulsed, and Germany itself was invaded in the spring of 1945. Eisenhower, many believed, could have captured Berlin, but his armies were busy enveloping one German force after another. Because the postwar zones of occupation—with Berlin inside the Russian zone—had already been approved at the **Yalta Conference** (*see*), he decided, according to an aide, that "the taking of Berlin would be a mere show, what he wanted to do was to end the war as quickly and economically in lives as possible." On May 7, 1945, General Alfred Jodl (1892?–1946), chief of the German Armed Forces Operations Staff, surrendered at a schoolhouse in Reims, France. Eisenhower was subsequently hailed by the Allies as a hero. He commanded the United States occupation forces in Germany until November, 1945, when he returned home to succeed Marshall as Chief of Staff. In 1946, he was elevated to the rank of five-star General of the Army. Eisenhower resigned from the post in February, 1948, and denying any interest in running for public office, retired from the army that May to become president of Columbia University. Within a few years, he was to change his mind and seek the Presidency. (*Entry continues in Volume 16.*)

F

FLETCHER, Frank Jack (1885–1973). As a task force commander of the United States Pacific Fleet during World War II, Fletcher played a major role in the battles of the Coral Sea and Midway (*see pp. 1293–1295*). Born in Iowa, Fletcher graduated from Annapolis in 1906. During World War I, he commanded the destroyer *Benham* and was awarded a Distinguished Ser-

vice Medal for protecting "vitally important convoys of troops and supplies" in the North Atlantic. By the time of America's entry into World War II, Fletcher, who had served peacetime duty both at sea and as a naval aide in Washington, D.C., was commander of a cruiser division in the Pacific. In the Battle of the Coral Sea (*see pp. 1292–1294*) in May, 1942—the first of the carrier battles that characterized much of the naval warfare in the Pacific Theater of Operations— he commanded a task force of American and Australian warships that included two large carriers, the *Yorktown,* which was badly damaged, and the *Lexington,* which was sunk. However, one enemy carrier was destroyed and another was disabled, thus checking the Japanese advance southward toward Australia. In the Battle of Midway that June, he commanded one of the two task forces, losing the *Yorktown.* The second task force, headed by Rear Admiral **Raymond A. Spruance** (*see*), sank four Japanese carriers. The battle marked Japan's first decisive naval defeat of the war. Fletcher, who was subsequently promoted to vice admiral, then commanded two of the three task forces engaged in the landings at Guadalcanal and Tulagi Islands on August 7–8, 1942 (*see pp. 1295–1296*). Later, he headed the Northwestern Sea Frontier and its replacement, the Alaskan Sea Frontier. A task force under his command was the first to penetrate the Sea of Okhotsk in March, 1945, bombarding the Kurile island of Paramushira. After the war ended, Fletcher, who had won two more Distinguished Service Medals for his services, took part in the occupation of Northern Japan. He returned to the United States in December, 1945, and the follow-

ing May became a member of the General Board of the Navy Department. In 1947, he was appointed chairman of that board, a position he held until his retirement one year later. At that time, he was transferred to the navy's retired list and advanced to the rank of full admiral.

FRANCO, Francisco (1892–1975). As chief of state, prime minister, and generalissimo of the armed forces. Franco has ruled Spain as an absolute dictator since 1939. Born Francisco Paulino Hermenegildo Teodulo Franco-Bahamonde at El Ferrol in the province of Galicia, Franco began his military career in 1907, enrolling at the infantry academy in Toledo. Following graduation in 1910, he volunteered to serve in Spanish Morocco. By 1920, he was deputy commander of the Span-

General Franco was depicted in 1965 as a hangman by a Communist artist.

ish foreign legion and three years later became commander. While in Morocco, he was credited with the final suppression of the Riff tribesmen. In 1927, Franco, by then a brigadier general, became director general of the military academy at Zaragoza. He remained in that post until

1931, when King Alphonso XIII (1886–1941) abdicated and the Spanish Republic was proclaimed. Because of his rightist views, Franco was transferred to the Balearic Islands off the coast of Spain in the Mediterranean and was later sent to Morocco. When a right-wing government came to power in 1935, Franco returned to Spain as chief of the general staff. However, the following year a leftist regime took control, and Franco was again "banished," to the Canary Islands in the Atlantic Ocean as military governor. At the beginning of an army revolt in July, 1936, he flew to Spanish Morocco, where he organized and brought back to Spain an army of foreign legionnaires and Moorish troops. Franco subsequently became the leader of the insurgent Nationalist forces. In 1937, he organized the Falange Party, and as *El Caudillo* (the leader) he led the revolt that became the Spanish Civil War (1936–1939). Aided by Nazi Germany and Italy, Franco fought a war of attrition against Republican forces in northwestern Spain. Despite Russian assistance and the aid of many volunteers from throughout the world, such as the Lincoln Brigade from the United States, the Republicans were finally forced to surrender Madrid on March 28, 1939, after a two-year siege. Franco installed himself as dictator, proclaiming that he was "Supreme Chief, responsible only before God and History." During World War II, Franco kept Spain nominally neutral, though his sympathies were with the Axis powers. After 1950, Franco established friendly relations with Western countries. He began receiving vast amounts of military and economic aid from the United States in 1953 in return for the establishment of American naval and air bases on Spanish soil. Two years later, Spain was admitted to the United Nations. During 1947, Franco officially reestablished the Spanish monarchy. By popular referendum he was given the right to remain in office for life and to select his successor. In 1966, the dictator presented a new constitution to the Spanish parliament that was designed to facilitate the passage of power from his hands to those of his successor. Three years later, he formally designated Prince Juan Carlos of Bourbon (born 1938) as the next chief of state and future king of Spain. Juan Carlos became head of the Spanish government when Franco died in 1975.

H

HALSEY, William Frederick, Jr. (1882–1959). One of the navy's most daring and colorful combat officers during World War II, "Bull" Halsey played a leading role in destroying Japanese naval power in the Pacific. The son of a navy career man, Halsey was born in Elizabeth, New Jersey, and graduated from Annapolis in 1904. During World War I, he commanded destroyers based at Queenstown, Ireland, escorted troop convoys, patrolled mine-infested waters, and was awarded the Navy Cross. His navy career progressed steadily during peacetime, and in 1937 Halsey, a proponent of naval air power, became commandant of the Pensacola Naval Air Station in Florida. He was promoted to vice admiral in 1940 and was named to head the Pacific Fleet's Aircraft Battle Force. When the Japanese made their surprise attack on Pearl Harbor on December 7, 1941, Halsey's carriers, returning from delivering planes to Wake Island, were the only major American warships to escape damage. Four months later, he commanded the fleet that accompanied the aircraft carrier *Hornet,* from which Colonel **James Doolittle** (*see*) made his famous air attack on Tokyo. That autumn, Halsey was given command of the entire South Pacific Fleet, and he commenced the Solomon Islands campaign (1942–1943). At Guadalcanal in November, 1942, Halsey's naval forces sank at least 23 enemy ships and made possible the island's conquest by American troops in February, 1943. Soon afterward, he was promoted to the rank of full admiral. From 1943 to 1944, Halsey's warships accounted for the loss of 4,800 enemy planes and nearly 150,000 casualties. On June 17, 1944, he was placed in command of the Third Fleet, and he began deploying ships to aid General **Douglas MacArthur** (*see*) in the recovery of the Philippines from the Japanese. In October, at the battle for Leyte Gulf, Halsey's formidable Third Fleet, composed of carriers and battleships, routed a Japanese carrier fleet. In doing so, however, Halsey left uncovered his escort carriers, which then bore the brunt of the main Japanese attack. Halsey, who had been advised against this maneuver, showed a stubborn single-mindedness again when in December, 1944, he took his ships into a typhoon zone and lost three destroyers and 150 planes. Although he was threatened with a court-martial, none was ever held because of his popularity with his men. Early in 1945, Halsey supported invading American soldiers during the Luzon landings and prevented the arrival of enemy reinforcements. He next brought the war to the home islands of Japan, in a carrier-based attack during July and August, 1945. His planes destroyed naval bases, land installations, and coastal cities, making good his vow to "Beat the hell out of the Japs, wherever they may be found." Halsey was subsequently promoted to the five-star rank of Admiral of the Fleet after the surrender of Japan. He retired from active duty in 1947 and spent the rest of his life in private business.

HITLER, Adolf (1889–1945). One of the most ruthless tyrants in the history of the world, Hitler founded the Third Reich and led Germany into World War II. The strutting, moustached *Führer* (leader) was the son of a minor Austrian customs official named Schickelgruber, who had changed his name to Hitler. Adolf Hitler traveled to Vienna in 1907, where he planned to become a great artist. Failing at that, he eked out an existence by designing and selling postcards and posters. Hitler went to Munich in 1913 and volunteered for the German infantry at the outbreak of World War I. He served four years, rose to the rank of corporal, and received the Iron Cross for bravery. Returning to Munich, Hitler joined the small German Workers Party. By 1921, he had assumed its leadership and reorganized it as the National Socialist German Workers Party (NSDAP), or the Nazi Party. The party promoted anti-Semitic racial nationalism and criticized the new German republic. Hitler organized brownshirted stormtroopers (known as SA) and black-shirted elite guards (SS) in preparation for a civil war. They defiantly thrust their right arms outward in the Nazi salute and shouted "Heil, Hitler" whenever he appeared. On November 9, 1923, the Nazis tried to seize control of the Bavarian government. The attempted coup failed, and Hitler was arrested and sentenced to five years in prison. He was paroled after serving only nine months. During his imprisonment, he wrote *Mein Kampf (My Struggle)*, an exposition of his political views and a preview of his future political actions that were to lead, he said, to 1,000 years of German rule. The book sold 10,000,000 copies and made Hitler wealthy. He was determined to achieve control of the government by legal means. He held mass rallies and gave spellbinding, emotional speeches in which he pledged to avenge World War I, smash the supposed power of Jews and Communists, and make · Germany the master of the world. The worldwide depression in 1929 gave added impetus to the Nazi movement. In 1932, Hitler ran for president of the republic. He was defeated, but the Nazis received more than 13,000,000 votes (37% of the total) and emerged as the largest single party in Germany. On January 30, 1933, President Paul von Hindenburg (1847–1934) asked Hitler to become chancellor. Hitler accepted and moved to consolidate his power. He eliminated Communist opposition by blaming it for the burning of the *Reichstag* (parliament building) on February 27, 1933. After establishing a Ministry of Propaganda and Enlightenment headed by Joseph Goebbels (1897–1945), he organized a nationwide secret police force—the *Geheime Staatspolizei*, or Gestapo—in April, 1934. The following June, he instituted a "blood purge" against his own stormtroopers to gain the support of the regular German army. He then set about rearming Germany. Determined to rule the world, Hitler allied himself with **Benito Mussolini** (*see*) of Italy and the Japanese government. He launched his conquest of Europe by annexing Austria in 1938 and then invading Czechoslovakia and Poland the following year (*see pp. 1265–1267*). The invasion of Poland brought Britain and France into the war, and the latter was soon conquered too. Against the advice of his army advisers, Hitler then invaded Russia. Stymied by his inability to subdue either Britain or Russia, Hitler increasingly took over control of the war strategy, becoming more and more suspicious of his own generals' competence and abilities. Hitler had already obtained complete political control of the nation. He had obtained a decree on February 28, 1933— the day after the *Reichstag* fire —that enabled him to suspend the civil liberties of his political opponents. He used this decree to help the Nazi Party win the elections of March, 1933—the last elections held while Hitler was in power—and he placed many of his opponents in "protective custody" at concentration camps. In June, 1934, he turned control of these camps over to Heinrich Himmler (1900–1945), head of the SS. When the so-called Nuremberg laws of September, 1935, deprived Jews of their German citizenship, thousands of Jews were arrested and sent to concentration camps. After World War II started, a policy of mass extermination was instituted. "Death camps" were established as the "final solution" to the Jewish problem. More than 3,000,000 people were killed in one such camp— Auschwitz, in southern Poland. Estimates of the total number killed range as high as 10,000,000. In July, 1944, when the tide of war had turned against Germany, a group of high-ranking military and civilian officials attempted to assassinate Hitler. Although wounded only slightly, Hitler— by now showing signs of severe mental instability and living on drugs—instituted a vindictive purge against the collaborators. Following the successful Allied landings on D-Day, June 6, 1944 (*see pp. 1275–1289*), German armies were gradually beaten back on two fronts until it became certain that further fighting was hopeless. On April 29, 1945, Hitler married his mistress, Eva Braun (1912–1945), in a massive bunker under the German chancellery in Berlin that he used for his headquarters. The following day, the couple committed suicide. Their bodies, by prearrangement, were burned with gasoline afterward. Difficulties in later identifying them led to speculation that Hitler might have escaped Germany's defeat and still be alive. However, in 1968, the Russian government disclosed that its troops had uncovered conclusive evidence of his death.

HOPKINS, Harry Lloyd (1890–1946).

During World War II, the frail but tireless Hopkins, a close personal friend of President **Franklin D. Roosevelt** (*see*), played a central role in formulating American strategy. Shortly after his graduation from Grinnell College in 1912, Iowa-born Hopkins entered social work in New York. He was employed by various welfare agencies in New York City until World War I, when he went to New Orleans as director of civilian relief and manager of the Southern division of the American Red Cross. Hopkins returned to New York in 1922 to resume his welfare work there, remaining until Roosevelt, then governor of New York, called him to Albany to oversee statewide relief activities during the Depression. When he became President in 1933, Roosevelt took Hopkins with him to Washington, D.C. As Federal Emergency Relief Ad-

WIDE WORLD

Harry Hopkins

ministrator (1933–1935) and head of the Works Progress Administration (1935–1938), Hopkins was called—with approval by some and in bitterness by others—the "world's biggest spender." He disbursed more than $10,000,000,000 to the hungry and homeless and to nearly 15,000,000 persons engaged in thousands of public projects created by the federal government to relieve unemployment during the Depression. Hopkins vigorously directed the repair, improvement, and building of 83,000 schools, 17,000 bridges, 3,000 water-supply systems, and many thousands of roads, recreational facilities, and sewer systems. In addition, he helped devise much of the pioneering social legislation of the New Deal. Hopkins spearheaded the drive for Roosevelt's unprecedented third-term nomina-

tion at the 1940 Democratic National Convention. After serving as Secretary of Commerce from 1938 to 1940, Hopkins, long in poor health, resigned from the cabinet. However, within a few months, Roosevelt asked him to assume the task of administering the $15,000,000,000 lend-lease program to aid war-wracked Allied nations in Europe (*see pp. 1269–1270*). He was also the President's most intimate wartime associate, representing him in missions to London in 1941 and 1942 and to Moscow in 1941. Accompanying Roosevelt to the major Allied meetings (*see* **Cairo, Casablanca, Teheran,** and **Yalta Conferences**), he won the respect of such world leaders as British Prime Minister **Winston Churchill** (*see*), who later said of Hopkins, "He always went to the root of the matter." Worn down by 12 strenuous years in Washington, Hopkins retired in July, 1945, less than three months after Roosevelt's death. That September, President **Harry S. Truman** (*see*) awarded him the Distinguished Service Medal for his contributions to Allied unity during the war.

HULL, Cordell (1871–1955).

As Secretary of State in the cabinet of President **Franklin D. Roosevelt** (*see*), Hull ran the State Department with intelligence and efficiency during the difficult era of the Great Depression and World War II (*see p. 1273*). Called by Roosevelt the father of the United Nations, Hull was awarded the Nobel Peace Prize in 1945 for his leadership in furthering international cooperation. Hull's dignified manner and quiet Southern drawl belied the fact that he was a shrewd politician who had made his way through rough-and-tumble local politics in his native Tennessee to national eminence. He studied law at Cumberland University for a single year before being admitted to the Tennessee bar in 1891. After serving in the state legislature (1893–1897), he led a company of volunteers to Cuba in 1898 during the Spanish-American War. Hull was appointed to a circuit-court judgeship in Tennessee in 1903, serving on the bench until his election to the House of Representatives four years later. During his many years in the House (1907–1921 and 1923–1931), Hull became known as an expert on matters of taxation and the tariff. He sponsored such key legislation as the federal income-tax law of 1913 and the federal inheritance-tax law of 1916, and he was a leader in the fight to reduce tariff barriers to promote freer international trade. Elected to the Senate in 1930, Hull resigned three years later to become Roosevelt's Secretary of State, a post he was to hold nearly 12 years—longer than any other person. Among Hull's notable achievements, in addition to his contributions to the founding of the United Nations (pp. 1311–1331), were his promotion of the good-neighbor policy toward Latin America and his sponsorship of a reciprocal trade act in 1934, by which he sought to better foreign relations through a lowering of tariff restrictions. Hull argued for American participation in the World Court, but isolationists in the Senate blocked this aim. Although he had supported United States neutrality in the European conflicts of the 1930s, he favored American aid to the Allies after 1939. In one of the most dramatic moments in American diplomatic history, Hull confronted the Japanese envoys in Washington, D.C., on December 7, 1941, at the very instant when Japanese planes were bombing Pearl Harbor (see pp. 1273–1274 and 1291). Hull

was more doubtful of Russian intentions than Roosevelt, but he supported the President's efforts to cooperate with **Joseph Stalin** (*see*) during the war. However, he was rankled at not being included in three important Allied meetings during World War II—the **Cairo, Casablanca, and Teheran Conferences** (*see all*). Hull resigned from the cabinet in 1944 because of failing health, but he continued to be consulted on foreign affairs by the State Department. His *Memoirs* were published in 1948.

I

IRON CURTAIN. *See* **Churchill, Winston.**

J

JACKSON, Robert Houghwout (1892–1954). Jackson, who was an Associate Justice of the Supreme Court from 1941 until his death, served (1945–1946) as chief prosecutor for the United States at the international trials of Nazi war criminals at Nuremberg, Germany. During the trials, he established a precedent for prosecuting war criminals on the basis of their having planned and conducted aggressive warfare. This new theory of international law was based on Jackson's statement that "No longer may a head of state consider himself outside the law, and impose inhuman acts on the peoples of the world." Born in Pennsylvania, Jackson studied at the Albany Law School and was admitted to the New York bar in 1913 before earning either a bachelor's or law degree. He later received his bachelor's from Chautauqua Institute, but he never did earn a law degree. He had established a successful practice in Jamestown, New

York, when in 1934 President **Franklin D. Roosevelt** (*see*) appointed him general counsel for the Bureau of Internal Revenue. In this capacity, Jackson initiated a $750,000 income-tax evasion case against Andrew W. Mellon (1855–1937), the onetime Secretary of the Treasury who had recently resigned as ambassador to Great Britain. Mellon had to pay the government the $750,000 but was absolved of any intent to defraud the government. Jackson subsequently served as special counsel (1935) for the Securities and Exchange Commission and as an Assistant Attorney General (1936–1938) in charge of the Antitrust Division. A strong supporter of Roosevelt's New Deal measures, he was appointed Solicitor General—the government's lawyer before the Supreme Court—in 1938. He argued 44 cases concerning the constitutionality of New Deal legislation, winning all but six. While serving as Attorney General (1940–1941), Jackson was an adviser in the negotiations that resulted in the exchange of 50 overage American destroyers for air and naval bases on British possessions in the Western Hemisphere. Shortly before the United States' entry into World War II in 1941, Roosevelt appointed Jackson to the Supreme Court. At the Nuremberg trials, his prosecution of 22 Nazi war criminals led to the sentencing of 12 to the gallows. These included Hans Frank (1900–1946), the head of civil administration in Polish territory after 1939; Wilhelm Frick (1877–1946), the German minister of the interior from 1933 to 1943; Colonel General Alfred Jodl (1892?–1946), the chief of staff; Gestapo chief Ernst Kaltenbrunner (1901–1946); Field Marshal Wilhelm Keitel (1882–1946), chief of the Supreme Command of the German Armed

On trial at Nuremberg were, from left, Goering, Hess, Karl Doenitz, Ribbentrop, Erich Raeder, Keitel, Baldur von Schirach, Kaltenbrunner, and Sauckel.

Forces; Alfred Rosenberg (1893–1946), the chief philosopher for the Nazis and the minister for the Eastern European nations conquered by Germany; Fritz Sauckel (1894–1946), the commissioner-general of manpower in occupied territories; Artur von Seyss-Inquart (1892–1946), a high Nazi official in Austria, Poland, and the Netherlands; Julius Streicher (1885–1946), the managing editor of *Der Sturmer* (1923–1946), a newspaper that incited anti-Semitic atrocities and championed the "propaganda of death"; and Foreign Minister Joachim von Ribbentrop (1893–1946). The 11th, Hermann Goering (1893–1946), a high Nazi official and the president of the council for war economy after 1940, committed suicide, and the 12th, Martin Bormann (1900–1945), a high Nazi leader, was reported dead in 1945 but was sentenced to death *in absentia*. Since then, there have been recurrent reports that he has been living in South America. Of the remaining 10 Nazis charged with war crimes, three were acquitted, three were given life sentences, and the rest were given prison sentences ranging from 10 to 20 years. Albert Speer (born 1905), Nazi armaments chief, was released

in 1966, leaving only the demented Rudolf Hess (1894–1987), once the third most powerful man in the Nazi regime, in Berlin's Spandau War Crimes Prison. President **Harry S. Truman** (*see*) awarded Jackson a Medal for Merit for his "extraordinary fidelity and exceptionally meritorious conduct" in prosecuting the Nazi leaders. Jackson's last judicial action was on May 17, 1954, when in spite of illness he appeared on the Supreme Court to emphasize its unanimity in announcing the outlawing of racial segregation in public schools. Jackson's writings include *The Struggle for Judicial Supremacy* (1941), *The Case Against the Nazi War Criminals* (1946), and *The Nürnberg Case* (1947).

K

KINKAID, Thomas Cassin (1888–1972). In October, 1944, Kinkaid and Admiral **William F. Halsey** (*see*) led the naval forces that nearly destroyed the Japanese navy in the Battle of Leyte Gulf. The son of a rear admiral, Kinkaid graduated from Annapolis in 1908 and served as a liaison officer with the British admiralty in World War I. In

peacetime, Kinkaid was trained as a gunnery officer and was the naval adviser to the American delegation at the Disarmament Conference in Geneva, Switzerland, in 1930. From 1938 to 1941, he was the naval attaché at the American embassies in Rome and Belgrade, Yugoslavia. Transferred to the Pacific Fleet after the United States entered World War II, Kinkaid commanded a task force in the Battles of the Coral Sea, Midway, and the Solomon Islands in 1942. The next year, he was named commander in chief of naval forces in the North Pacific and in November, 1943, became commander of the Seventh Fleet. Kinkaid and Halsey, who commanded the Third Fleet, led the naval support for the troops commanded by General **Douglas MacArthur** (*see*) in the Philippines campaign in October, 1944. In the Leyte Gulf battle, Kinkaid's six battleships—all but one of which had been sunk or damaged during the Japanese attack on Pearl Harbor three years earlier—annihilated 12 Japanese warships in Surigao Strait, allowing only one enemy destroyer to escape. In April, 1945, Kinkaid was promoted to admiral, and that September he represented the navy and accepted the Japanese surrender in South Korea. After the war, Kinkaid was placed in command of the Atlantic Reserve Fleet.

L

LEAHY, William Daniel (1875–1959). After serving in the United States Navy for more than 40 years, Leahy became Chief of Staff to President **Franklin D. Roosevelt** (*see*) during World War II. Born in Hampton, Iowa, Leahy graduated from Annapolis in 1897, and the following year he went to sea as a midshipman on board the *Oregon* and participated in the Spanish-American War. While serving as captain of the dispatch boat *Dolphin* in World War I, Leahy had Assistant Secretary of the Navy Roosevelt for a passenger, and the two became good friends. After Roosevelt became President, he made Leahy Chief of Naval Operations and a full admiral in 1937, although Leahy was forced to give up the post in 1939 because he had reached the mandatory retirement age of 64. He was then named governor of Puerto Rico, where he served until 1940, when the President appointed him ambassador to the puppet government of Henri Pétain (1856–1951) at Vichy, France. He was recalled to America in 1942 and became President Roosevelt's Chief of Staff. In his role as senior military adviser, Leahy attended nearly all the major international conferences during the war, including the controversial **Yalta Conference** (*see*) in February, 1945. Holding the five-star rank of Admiral of the Fleet at the time of Roosevelt's death in April, 1945, Leahy continued in the same capacity under President **Harry S. Truman** (*see*). He accompanied Truman to the **Potsdam Conference** (*see*) in July, 1945, and helped reorganize

William D. Leahy

the nation's armed services under the unified Department of Defense. During this period, he was criticized for underestimating the destructive capability of the atomic bomb (*see* **Manhattan Project**), which he referred to as "a lot of hooey." Leahy retired from public life in 1949.

M

MacARTHUR, Douglas (1880–1964). Criticized by some for his abundant self-confidence and stubbornness but a hero to the men he led, MacArthur was one of the most brilliant commanders of modern times. Sporting a corncob pipe, sunglasses, and a battered campaign cap and possessing a gift for memorable language, he was also one of America's most colorful military figures. He directed the Allied victory in the Pacific Theater in World War II and then took charge (1945–1951) of the demilitarization and rebuilding of Japan during the Allied occupation. During the Korean War, he commanded all United Nations forces in Korea until 1951, when he was relieved of duty by President **Harry S. Truman** (*see*) for publicly opposing the administration's war strategy. MacArthur was born at an army post near Little Rock, Arkansas, the son of Lieutenant General Arthur MacArthur (1845–1912), who had served with distinction in the Civil War and the Spanish-American War. After a youth spent at frontier forts throughout the West, where his father fought in Indian campaigns, MacArthur won an appointment to West Point in 1899. He graduated in 1903 with the highest scholastic record of any cadet in the preceding 25 years. Commissioned in the Corps of Engineers, he was assigned to duty

in the Philippines (1903–1904) and Japan (1905–1906) and then served (1906–1907) as an aide to President Theodore Roosevelt (1858–1919). After assignment to the army general staff (1913–1917), MacArthur became Chief of Staff and later commander of the famous Forty-second (Rainbow) Infantry Division in 1918. As a brigadier general, he fought in France in all the major battles of World War I involving American troops and was twice wounded. Appointed superintendent of West Point (1919–1922), MacArthur modernized the military academy and raised it from being a "trade school" to full collegiate status. After holding various commands in the Philippines and the United States from 1922 to 1930, MacArthur was named Army Chief of Staff in 1930 by President Herbert Hoover (1874–1964). Over the next five years, he succeeded—despite the meager funds available during the Depression—in strengthening and updating the army. In the summer of 1932, MacArthur was ordered by Hoover to disperse several thousand disgruntled World War I veterans who were conducting a "Bonus March" on Washington. MacArthur returned to the Far East in 1935 to organize the defense of the Philippines. He retired from the United States Army two years later to become field marshal of the Philippine army. However, he was recalled to active duty in 1941 on the eve of World War II and made commander of American forces in the Far East. MacArthur directed a stubborn defense of the Philippines against Japanese assault, but with defeat threatening in March, 1942, he was evacuated by a PT boat to Australia, vowing, "I shall return." In command of all Allied forces in the Southwest Pacific, MacArthur turned to the offensive, relentlessly driving back the Japanese in the South Pacific (*see pp. 1298–1301*). On October 30, 1944, MacArthur fulfilled his promise to the Philippine people by wading ashore at Leyte. Two months later, he was promoted to the five-star rank of General of the Army. MacArthur's planned invasion of the Japanese home islands became unnecessary after atomic bombs were dropped on Hiroshima and Nagasaki in August, 1945 (*see* **Manhattan Project**). On September 2, 1945, on the battleship *Missouri* in Tokyo Bay, MacArthur accepted the formal, unconditional surrender of Japan (*see p. 1307 and back endsheet*). For the next five years, he directed—with a rigid but statesmanlike hand—the dismantling of the Japanese military machine and the conversion of Japan to a peacetime economy. After North Korea invaded South Korea in June, 1950, the United Nations Security Council voted to aid the besieged republic, and Mac-Arthur was named commanding general of U.N. forces by President Truman. That September, MacArthur directed the daring amphibious landings at the port of Inchon in South Korea and the counterattack that drove the Communist armies back across the 38th parallel into North Korea. However, MacArthur's intelligence network had erred in concluding that the Chinese Communists would not enter the war, and in late 1950 his forces were thrown back by a massive Chinese offensive. The following spring, with the war at a virtual stalemate, MacArthur publicly advocated the bombing of Chinese bases and supply lines across the Yalu River in Manchuria, a strategy that seriously conflicted with administration policy. On April 11, 1951, Truman relieved MacArthur of his

command and replaced him with General **Matthew B. Ridgway** (*see*). MacArthur's 52-year military career thus ended in a sensational dispute over the limits of military authority. He received a hero's welcome upon his return to the United States— his first visit in 15 years—and expressed his views before a joint session of Congress on April 19, 1951, concluding dramatically with this quotation from an old army song, "Old soldiers never die—they just fade away." MacArthur was considered briefly to head the Republican Presidential ticket in 1952, but the nomination went to General **Dwight D. Eisenhower** (*see*). From 1952 until his death, MacArthur lived in New York City, where he was chairman of the board of Remington Rand, Inc. (now Sperry-Rand).

MANHATTAN PROJECT. Created on August 13, 1942, and placed officially under the code name Manhattan Engineer District, the Manhattan Project was the United States' crash program to develop the atomic bomb. The research was centered in three different government-supported laboratories. Arthur H. Compton (1892–1962) headed the University of Chicago team, Ernest O. Lawrence (1901–1958) led a team at the University of California, and **Harold C. Urey** (*see*) supervised work at Columbia University. Each was working on a different method to produce fissionable materials that were capable of releasing enormous amounts of explosive energy. The famed Italian-born physicist Enrico Fermi (1901–1954), who was working at the Chicago laboratory, initiated the first self-sustaining nuclear chain reaction in December, 1942. After his success, a plutonium-production plant was constructed in Hanford, Washington. Larger

The "Little Boy" dropped at Hiroshima was a mere 10 feet long.

plants to manufacture fissionable materials were constructed in Oak Ridge, Tennessee. The responsibility for the design of the bomb was given to physicist **J. Robert Oppenheimer** (*see*), who had his headquarters in Los Alamos, New Mexico. Brigadier General Leslie R. Groves (1896–1970) was the administrative chief of the project and maintained elaborate security precautions. A maximum-security city housing 25,000 workers was built in Oak Ridge. Nearly $2,000,000,000 was spent on the project, and more than 125,000 people at different locations were employed, though only a handful were aware of the nature of the project. President **Franklin D. Roosevelt** did not even tell his Secretary of State, **Cordell Hull,** or his Vice-President, **Harry S. Truman** (*see all*). On July 16, 1945, three months after Roosevelt's death, a plutonium bomb was detonated in the desert near Alamogordo, New Mexico. Truman, now President, was informed of the project's success while attending the **Potsdam Conference** (*see*). He decided to use the bomb against the Japanese if they failed to accept the surrender ultimatum that was issued by the Allies on July 26, while he was still at the conference. When the Japanese did not surrender, despite warnings of "utter destruction," Colonel

Paul W. Tibbets, commander of the B-29 bomber *Enola Gay,* was ordered to take off from Tinian Island in the Marianas on August 6. An atomic bomb, called Little Boy, was on board. Tibbets and his crew did not know the nature of the bomb, and even the scientists could not be certain that it would explode, because unlike the plutonium bomb that had been tested, this one was composed of uranium-235. At 9:15 A.M., the bomb was dropped on Hiroshima. It exploded 2,000 feet above the city in a huge flash of light that dissolved into an immense, mushroom-shaped cloud rising to an altitude of 40,000 feet. An hour and a half later and 360 miles away, the crew could still look back and see the cloud. Nearly 40,000 people were killed instantly, more than 20,000 others eventually died of wounds and radiation illness, and 60,000 people were injured. When the Japanese did not capitulate, a plutonium bomb, nicknamed Fat Man, was dropped on Nagasaki on August 9. Approximately 36,000 people were killed and 60,000 injured. Japan sued for peace the next day. On January 1, 1947, the civilian-controlled Atomic Energy Commission assumed the responsibilities held by the Manhattan Project and set about developing peaceful uses for nuclear power in addition to nuclear weapons.

MARSHALL, George Catlett (1880–1959). One of America's most respected military leaders and strategists, Marshall, who was Chief of Staff of the American army during World War II, is often called the architect of victory. In addition, as Secretary of State afterward, he devised the Marshall Plan for the economic recovery of war-torn Europe. Born in Pennsylvania, Marshall graduated from the

For French farmers, the Marshall Plan provided new farm equipment.

Virginia Military Institute in 1901. One of the few non-West Pointers to achieve high rank, Marshall spent 15 years in the peacetime army as a lieutenant. His promotion to captain did not come until July, 1916, after he had been commended as "the greatest military genius of America since Stonewall Jackson" for his part in war games earlier that year. In July, 1917, Marshall left with the first convoy sent to France as a member of the General Staff. Marshall earned the praise of the American Expeditionary Force commander, General John J. Pershing (1860–1948), and became his aide in 1919. He accompanied Pershing to Washington, D.C., when Pershing was named Army Chief of Staff in 1921. Marshall's brilliant reorganization (1927–1932) of the Infantry School at Fort Benning, Georgia, was followed by a series of commands in which he consistently distinguished himself as a strategist in simulated war maneuvers. In August, 1939, he was chosen Chief of Staff, over 34 officers senior to him, by President **Franklin D. Roosevelt** (*see*). At Marshall's urging, Congress enacted measures that created the largest peacetime army in Ameri-

can history—about 1,000,000 men—by the fall of 1941. Marshall's success in World War II was in part due to his coolness under pressure. "I have no feelings," he told an acquaintance, "except a few which I reserve for Mrs. Marshall." Ignoring seniority, Marshall picked outstanding subordinates from all ranks of the officer corps. Generals **Dwight D. Eisenhower, George S. Patton, Jr.,** and **Walter Bedell Smith** (*see all*) were all promoted over senior men. Marshall himself was elevated to the newly created post of General of the Army when he rejected the idea of being named a marshal because he "did not care to be called Marshal Marshall." He accompanied Roosevelt to all the Allied conferences during the war (*see* **Cairo, Casablanca, Teheran,** and **Yalta Conference**), and it was Marshall's proposal, prevailing over Churchill's plan to attack the "soft underbelly of Europe" from the Mediterranean Sea, that led to the invasion across the English Channel on D-Day, June 6, 1944 (*see pp. 1275–1289*). Marshall retired shortly after the war ended in 1945, but President **Harry S. Truman** (*see*) asked him to go to China to prevent civil war between Communist forces and the Nationalist armies of **Chiang Kai-shek** (*see*). Marshall returned in January, 1947, and reported his mission a failure. Within a month, he was appointed Secretary of State. The essential goal of Truman's foreign policy, which became known as the Truman Doctrine, was to contain Soviet expansion by extending American economic and military aid to all free nations in the world. Marshall's proposal to broaden this policy, officially known as the European Recovery Program, is better known as the Marshall Plan. It marked the first time a victorious nation had ever restored prosperity to its defeated enemy. Marshall received the Nobel Peace Prize for the Marshall Plan in 1953. After resigning as Secretary of State in December, 1948, Marshall subsequently served as Secretary of Defense for a year during the Korean War before retiring.

MONTGOMERY, Bernard Law

(1887–1976). A flinty, outspoken British military leader, "Monty," as his soldiers called him, became a national idol in October, 1942, when he won the first major British victory of World War II, the Battle of El Alamein in Egypt. He later played a crucial role in the Allied victory in Europe. A graduate (1908) of Sandhurst, Britain's West Point, Montgomery was a lieutenant general at the outbreak of World War II. He commanded the Third Division in France until the British Expeditionary Forces were evacuated from Dunkirk in the early summer of 1940. In December, 1941, Montgomery was given command of the South Eastern Army in England, and in August, 1942, he became commander of the Eighth Army in North Africa. The following October, with his famed Desert Rats reinforced by American tanks, he decisively defeated the *Afrika Korps* under Field Marshal **Erwin Rommel** (*see*). He drove the Germans more than 1,750 miles across Africa into Tunisia and continued to lead the Eighth Army until the Axis powers capitulated in Africa in May, 1943. Montgomery then led that army into Sicily and Italy (September-December, 1943) and subsequently helped plan the Allied invasion of France. He played major roles in the Normandy campaign and in the Battle of the Bulge, and on May 4, 1945, a few days before Germany surrendered uncondi-

tionally, he accepted the surrender of half a million Germans. After the war, Montgomery, who had been promoted to the rank of field marshal in 1944, served as commander in chief of the British Army of Occupation in Germany (1945–1946), and in January, 1946, he was created Viscount Montgomery of Alamein. He later served (1948–1951) as chief of the commanders in chief committee of the Brussels Treaty Powers—Belgium, Britain, France, Luxembourg, and the Netherlands—and as Deputy Supreme Allied Commander (1951–1958) in Europe. Montgomery retired in 1958 after 50 years of military service.

Bernard L. Montgomery

His publications include *El Alamein to the River Sangro* (1948), *The Memoirs of Field Marshal Montgomery* (1958), and *History of Warfare* (1968).

MORGENTHAU, Henry, Jr.

(1891–1967). As Secretary of the Treasury under President **Franklin D. Roosevelt** (*see*) for 11 years, Morgenthau was responsible for reestablishing the stability of the American economy during the Depression and later raising the funds to pay the costs of prosecuting World War II. The New York-born statesman briefly studied architecture at Cornell University, but his

interest soon turned to agriculture. In 1913, he purchased a large farm in Duchess County, New York, which became his permanent home. Two years later, a neighbor, Franklin D. Roosevelt, invited young Morgenthau to lunch at Hyde Park. The invitation began a friendship that was to continue until Roosevelt's death in 1945. In 1922, Morgenthau purchased the weekly magazine, *The American Agriculturist*. As its publisher until 1933, he promoted methods of scientific farming and conservation. When Roosevelt was elected governor of New York in 1928, he appointed Morgenthau chairman of the Agricultural Advisory Commission and in 1930 conservation commissioner of the state. Following his election as President two years later, Roosevelt named Morgenthau chairman of the Federal Farm Board, and in 1933 Morgenthau organized the Farm Credit Administration. At that time, the need for banking credit was a major problem for hundreds of thousands of farmers facing foreclosure on their mortgages. Morgenthau expanded agricultural credit and within a seven-month period in 1933 saw that $100,000,000 was lent to farmers at low interest rates. To raise agricultural prices, he supported a gold-purchase program, which resulted in the devaluation of the dollar late in 1933. That autumn, Roosevelt appointed Morgenthau acting Secretary of the Treasury, and in 1934, Secretary. For the next 11 years, Morgenthau fought for a balanced budget and international monetary cooperation. He purchased and sold gold, dollars, and foreign currencies on the international market. As a result of his monetary policies, the dollar became the soundest currency in circulation in the world. Two years before the

United States' entry into World War II, Morgenthau established a division in the Treasury Department to handle the sale of American arms to France and Britain. He also strongly promoted the sale of war bonds, raising billions of dollars in bond drives. Then, concerned with postwar economic problems, Morgenthau was active in the establishment of the World Bank and the International Monetary Fund in 1944. As the war drew to a close, he suggested a plan to prevent Germany from ever again rising to a position of military power. His proposal called for the division of that nation into several agrarian, non-industrial states. The so-called Morgenthau Plan, though considered by the Allied leaders, was never accepted. Soon after President **Harry S. Truman** (*see*) took office in 1945, Morgenthau resigned his post. By then, he had raised nearly $450,000,000,000 through taxes and loans—more money than all the previous Treasury Secretaries together in American history. Morgenthau served (1951–1954) as chairman of the American Financial and Development Corporation for Israel. Throughout his years as Secretary of the Treasury, the statesman had kept a detailed diary, a study of which was published in 1959 by John Morton Blum of Yale University under the title *From the Morgenthau Diaries*.

MUSSOLINI, Benito (1883–1945). The Fascist dictator of Italy from 1922 to 1943, Mussolini allied his country with Germany and Japan in World War II. The editor of several Socialist · Party newspapers, Mussolini had founded in Milan in 1919 the Fascio di Combattimento, which later became the Fascist Party. As its head, he seized control of the government in

1922, with the backing of World War I veterans and businessmen alarmed by strikes and social unrest. Mussolini gained support of the Roman Catholic Church by recognizing the sovereignty of the State of Vatican City in 1929. Maintaining strict discipline in his political party, Mussolini—who was called Il Duce (The Leader)—eliminated opposition parties and newspapers and became aggressive in foreign affairs. At first cool toward **Adolf Hitler** (*see*), Mussolini sent Italian troops to Austria in 1934 to frustrate Germany's attempt to take over the Vienna government. The following year, Italian troops invaded and conquered Ethiopia in order to expand the Italian colony in northeastern Africa. This caused Britain and France to turn against him, and Mussolini then formed the Rome-Berlin Axis with the only national leader who would support his Ethiopian conquest, Hitler. Following Hitler's example, Mussolini sent troops and planes to aid **Francisco Franco** (*see*) in the Spanish Civil War (1936–1939). Then in 1938, he supported Hitler's annexation of Austria and Czechoslovakia, and he himself annexed Albania for Italy in 1939. That same year, Mussolini signed a formal military alliance with Hitler (*see p. 1267*) but waited until France was nearly defeated in June, 1940, before declaring war. The failure of Italian armies in Greece and Africa, the imminent invasion of Italy by the Allies, and Hitler's refusal to use German troops to defend Italy led to a revolt within the Fascist Party in 1943. Mussolini was arrested and imprisoned in July, 1943, and Italy sued for peace. German paratroopers rescued him that September, and Mussolini set up a puppet Fascist government in northern Italy. In April, 1945, when German

resistance collapsed, Mussolini was captured by Italian partisans. After being shot, kicked and beaten, he was hanged by his feet with his mistress in a public square.

N

NIMITZ, Chester William (1885–1966). Nimitz was Commander in Chief of the United States Pacific Fleet during World War II. Born in Texas, he graduated from Annapolis in 1905, and during World War I was chief of staff to the commander of the Atlantic Fleet's submarine force. Nimitz established the nation's first Naval Reserve Officers Training Corps (NROTC) in 1926 at the University of California. As captain of the cruiser *Augusta* in 1935, he first met President **Franklin D. Roosevelt** (*see*) while on maneuvers. Nimitz was promoted to rear admiral in 1938, and a year later was appointed chief of the navy's bureau of navigation. After the attack on Pearl Harbor on December 7, 1941, Roosevelt named Nimitz commander in chief of the Pacific Fleet, promoting him over 28 senior officers. The Allied command divided the South Pacific into two general strategic areas (*see p. 1299*), with Nimitz commanding all Allied naval, land, and air forces in one sector and General **Douglas MacArthur** (*see*) in the other. In June, 1942, Nimitz directed the successful defense of the Hawaiian Islands at the Battle of Midway, checking the Japanese offensive in the Pacific. That August, he and MacArthur launched a joint offensive. From his headquarters at Pearl Harbor, Nimitz, who favored a policy of seizing only strategic Japanese-held islands rather than all of them, skillfully directed the invasions in the Central Pacific (*see pp.*

1298–1301). In 1944, he was promoted to the rank of five-star admiral. By 1945, his Pacific Fleet, which had been nearly destroyed at Pearl Harbor, was the greatest naval force ever assembled by one nation. On September 2, 1945, Nimitz signed the Japanese surrender document aboard his flagship, the *Missouri,* in Tokyo Bay (*see p. 1307 and back endsheet*). Two months later, he was appointed Chief of Naval Operations, serving in that post until 1947, when he retired from active duty. Nimitz headed an unsuccessful United Nations commission to settle the India-Pakistan dispute over Kashmir in 1949.

NUREMBERG TRIALS. *See* **Jackson, Robert.**

O

O'NEILL, Eugene (1888–1953). Recognized as one of the world's most outstanding playwrights, O'Neill revitalized the American stage by bringing to it serious dramas whose characters attained tragic dimensions. O'Neill, who was the son of the popular romantic actor James O'Neill (1847–1920), was born in New York City. He toured as a child with his father's theatrical troupe, receiving only a sporadic education and briefly attending Princeton University (1906–1907). Over the next few years, O'Neill prospected for gold in Honduras and traveled as a seaman to South America and South Africa. While convalescing from a near-fatal case of tuberculosis in 1912, O'Neill turned to drama to convey his impressions of life at sea and the oppressed people he had encountered on his voyages. In the next two years, he wrote a number of plays, including the one-act drama *Bound East for*

Cardiff. He subsequently studied modern dramatic technique at Harvard (1914–1915) and then lived in New York City's Greenwich Village among the social outcasts who were the prototypes of characters in his later tragedies. In 1916, O'Neill became associated with the Provincetown Players, a famed theater group that produced some of his early dramas. His years of apprenticeship ended with the 1920 production of *Beyond the Horizon,* a tragedy set in New England, which established O'Neill as America's foremost playwright and won him the first of four Pulitzer Prizes in 1921. This play was followed by other dramas with themes of tragic frustration, such as *Anna Christie* (1921), the winner of his second Pulitzer Prize in 1922; *Desire Under the Elms* (1924); and the six-hour-long, nine-act *Strange Interlude* (1927), which won a Pulitzer Prize in 1928. O'Neill also wrote complicated symbolic plays, such as *The Great God Brown* (1926), an attack on the drive for material possessions in modern life. One of O'Neill's most impressive works, *Mourning Becomes Electra* (1931), retells the ancient Greek tragedy known as the Orestean trilogy in contemporary terms. In it, O'Neill dealt with the theme of man's belief that he can defy the gods, and as in all his major plays, he depicted characters who search for peace within themselves and with their surroundings. In 1936, O'Neill was awarded the Nobel Prize for literature, the only American dramatist to be thus honored. He wrote no new plays from 1934 until 1946, when he completed *The Iceman Cometh,* which is generally considered to be his masterpiece. Based on the author's Greenwich Village experiences, the play is set in a saloon inhabited by a group of

Eugene O'Neill

drunken derelicts who manage to survive from day to day on their pipe dreams, until one day their illusions are shattered. When O'Neill died, he left in manuscript form the autobiographical *Long Day's Journey Into Night,* which was derived from the author's 1912 bout with tuberculosis. It was awarded a Pulitzer Prize for drama four years after his death. He also left portions of a projected play cycle about the fortunes of an American family from colonial times down to the present. Of these, *A Touch of the Poet* and *More Stately Mansions* were produced in 1960 and 1962, respectively.

P

PATTON, George Smith, Jr. (1885–1945). A flamboyant figure who always wore pearl-handled revolvers into combat, Patton was the American field commander that German generals most feared. He led three major assaults in the European Theater of Operations during World War II. Born into a wealthy family in California, Patton graduated from West Point in 1909 and became a cavalry officer. In 1916, he became aide-de-camp to General John J. Pershing (1860–1948) during the unsuccessful 11-month search in Mexico for the bandit Pancho Villa (1877–1923). The following year, he went to France, where he led the first American tanks into battle at Saint-Mihiel and the Argonne. After the Armistice in 1918, Patton brightened his next 22 years in the peacetime army by living lavishly on his inherited income—even keeping a string of polo ponies. When the United States began to rearm in 1940–1941, he was promoted to major general. After America entered World War II, the Supreme Allied Commander in Europe, **Dwight D. Eisenhower**

George S. Patton, Jr.

(*see*), chose the aggressive Patton to lead the first Allied offensive. Patton took the beach at Casablanca, but Eisenhower's secret negotiations with Admiral Jean Louis Darlan (1881–1942), head of the collaborationist French in North Africa, caused the North African French to stop fighting within a few days. Patton was next given command of the invasion of Sicily in July, 1943. On August 3, exhausted by the strain of the costly victories in Sicily that were earning him the nickname Old Blood and Guts, Patton slapped an unwounded enlisted man who was waiting to be admitted to a hospital. The

soldier was, in fact, suffering from battle fatigue, malaria, and chronic diarrhea. A similar incident a week later resulted in a severe reprimand from Eisenhower and was widely publicized. Nevertheless, with preparations for D-Day (*see pp. 1275–1289*) under way, Eisenhower placed Patton in command of the Third Army. In the last days of July, 1944, his armored division began a dash through France, reaching the German border so fast that supplies had to be air-dropped to him. During the Battle of the Bulge that winter, Patton's speed in moving his armored units to relieve Bastogne assured the Allied victory. In March, 1945, the Third Army became the first major force to cross the Rhine. When the Germans surrendered in May, 1945, Patton became military commander of Bavaria. After American reporters learned that Patton had not removed all former Nazis from local government posts, the general was baited by a journalist into comparing the Nazis to American political parties. Patton was promptly removed from command. Although a four-star general, he was given a "paper" army, whose sole function was to compile a historical journal of the fighting from D-Day to the final surrender. He died following an automobile accident in Germany.

POTSDAM CONFERENCE. After Germany's unconditional surrender in May, 1945, a conference was held at Potsdam, near Berlin, to lay the basis for a permanent peace settlement. President **Harry S. Truman** of the United States and Premier **Joseph Stalin** of Russia (*see both*) attended from July 17 through August 2. Prime Minister **Winston Churchill** of Great Britain was replaced by the newly elected prime minister, **Clement**

R. Attlee (*see both*), midway through the conference (*see p. 1335*). On July 26, 1945, the Potsdam Declaration was issued. It called for Japan's unconditional surrender and promised humane peace terms and "complete and utter destruction" to Japan if she refused. Generalissimo **Chiang Kai-shek** (*see*) of China signed the declaration, but Stalin did not, because Russia had not yet declared war on Japan. On July 17, Truman had been informed of the first successful atomic-bomb test, but the threat of an atomic attack was not mentioned in the declaration. Russian troops were moving toward the Far Eastern front, and the agreement for Russia to enter the war against Japan was reaffirmed at Potsdam. The chief problem at the conference was what to do with Germany. A blueprint for the control of Germany was issued on August 2, 1945. Germany and Austria were to be administered by an Allied control council of American, British, French, and Russian generals in charge of four zones. Berlin and Vienna, both far inside the Russian zones, would be "free cities," also administered in four zones. The zones were to last no longer than the Allied occupation. The economy of Germany was to be coordinated but rechanneled into agricultural and nonmilitary production. Reparations were to be credited to the victors on a percentage basis, and each Ally would take reparations from the zone it was administering. In addition, Nazi leaders were to be tried as war criminals (*see* **Robert Jackson**), and 6,500,000 Germans living in Eastern Europe were to be relocated inside Germany. Russia and the United States agreed to liberate Korea jointly, a decision that doomed Korean independence as promised at the **Cairo Conference** (*see*). Some crucial matters, such as the reconstruction of Poland, were left to be settled at a later peace conference, which was never held. Many issues of the subsequent cold war can be traced to the unsettled issues or broken agreements of the Potsdam Conference.

R

RANDOLPH, Asa Philip (1889–1979). A prominent black labor leader who has been called black labor's champion because of his lifelong work to end discrimina-

Randolph and Eleanor Roosevelt fought job discrimination in 1946.

tion, A. Philip Randolph has also been instrumental in the ending of racial barriers in America's armed forces. Born in Florida, Randolph attended the College of the City of New York while working as an elevator operator, waiter, and porter. He then worked as a writer and editor of *The Messenger*, a radical black magazine he helped found in 1917. That same year, he organized a small union of elevator operators in New York City, and in 1921 he ran unsuccessfully for the office of New York secretary of state on the Socialist ticket. Randolph believed that because the Pullman-car porters were not unionized, they were among the most exploited members of the Negro

labor force. Accordingly, in August, 1925, he began a campaign to organize a union for them, and although not a porter himself, he was elected its president and organizer. Because of heavy opposition from the Pullman Company, it took Randolph 12 years to win official recognition for the Brotherhood of Sleeping Car Porters. Finally, in 1937, the union negotiated a contract with the Pullman Company providing for pay increases, shorter hours, and overtime pay for its employees. Randolph organized a massive march-on-Washington movement in 1941, which threatened a demonstration in the capital to protest job discrimination. The movement hastened the creation that year of the Fair Employment Practices Committee, which was originally created as a wartime measure to curb discrimination in war-production and government jobs. Eventually, many local and state laws against race restrictions in employment were enacted. In 1948, largely because of Randolph's work to end segregation in the armed forces, President **Harry S. Truman** (*see*) issued an executive order ending segregation in the military services. Until then, blacks in the navy were largely limited to steward duties, and segregated units still existed in the army. In 1957, he was elected vice-president of the A.F.L.-C.I.O.

RIDGWAY, Matthew Bunker (born 1895). As commander of the famed Eighty-second Airborne Division during World War II, Ridgway parachuted with his men in the successful Allied invasion of Sicily, Italy, and France. Later, during the Korean War, he assumed command of the United States Eighth Army, after Lieutenant General Walton H. Walker (1889–1950) was killed in a jeep crash. He subsequently

became commander of all United Nations forces in Korea when General **Douglas MacArthur** was relieved of duty by President **Harry S. Truman** (*see both*). Born in Virginia, Ridgway held numerous military assignments between his graduation from West Point in 1917 and his appointment to command the Eighty-second Infantry (later Airborne) Division in 1942. During the 1920s, he was an instructor at West Point and served in various command and administrative posts in the United States, China, and Nicaragua. The following decade, his duties took him to the Panama Canal Zone, the Philippine Islands, Brazil, and the United States. He graduated from the Command and General Staff School in 1935 and the Army War College in 1937. At the outbreak of World War II, Ridgway was working in the plans division of the War Department. In mid-1942, he took command of the Eighty-second and the following year led his division in the first major paratrooper operation in American military history, during the invasion of Sicily. After participating in the ensuing Italian campaign, Ridgway and his division spearheaded the airborne assault behind enemy lines during the Normandy invasion (*see pp. 1275–1289*). After August of 1944, Ridgway was commander of the Eighteenth Airborne Corps in fighting in Belgium and Germany. Between the end of the war and his assignment to Korea in 1950, Ridgway held various key posts in the Mediterranean, the Caribbean, at the United Nations, and in Washington, D. C. As commander of United Nations forces in Korea, Ridgway directed offensives that drove the Communist armies back across the 38th parallel into North Korea, and he arranged the beginning of truce negotiations. Ridgway briefly succeeded (1952–1953) General **Dwight D. Eisenhower** (*see*) in Paris as Supreme Commander of the Allied Powers in Europe and then served as Army Chief of Staff (1953–1955). He retired from active duty in 1955 to become an executive with the Mellon Institute for Industrial Research in Pittsburgh. His *Soldier Memoirs* was published in 1956, and his *Korean War* in 1967.

ROMMEL, Erwin (1891–1944). Known as the Desert Fox, Rommel was the legendary commander of Germany's renowned lightninglike armored force, the *Afrika Korps*. He began his military career in 1910 as an officer cadet in the One Hundred Twenty-fourth Infantry Regiment. A lieutenant at the outbreak of World War I, he served in France, Rumania, and Italy. Rommel later became a military instructor (1935–1938). Made a full colonel in 1938, he was appointed chief of the German War Academy. Soon afterward, **Adolf Hitler** (*see*) put him in command of his honor-guard battalion. In this capacity, Rommel became responsible for Hitler's personal safety during the German invasions of Czechoslovakia in 1938 and Poland in 1939. The following year, Rommel, now a major general, commanded the Seventh Panzer Division during the German invasion of France. In 1941, when it appeared that the Italians were losing the struggle for control of North Africa, Hitler sent Rommel to Libya with three divisions to stop the British. In March, 1941, the Desert Fox launched an offensive that drove the British back to Egypt. With the exception of Tobruk, the entire Libyan coast was under his control in less than three weeks. For the next 14 months, the war in North

Erwin Rommel

Africa was a seesaw affair across the desert. "Rommel, Rommel, Rommel!" said British Prime Minister **Winston Churchill** (*see*). "What else matters but beating him!" By the late spring of 1942, however, Rommel succeeded in capturing Tobruk and was promoted to field marshal. That summer, Churchill put General **Bernard L. Montgomery** (*see*) in command of the Eighth Army. Under Montgomery's direction, the British overwhelmed the Germans at El Alamein. Rommel, in Germany on sick leave at the time, rushed back to the front but was too late to stave off the defeat. Following the Allied invasion of North Africa, Rommel was forced to retreat 1,750 miles back across the desert. Upon his return to Germany, Rommel was put in command of Army Group B in northern Italy to hold Italy after the overthrow of **Benito Mussolini** (*see*). In November, 1943, he was sent to inspect the coastal defenses from Denmark to Spain. He found them inadequate, but feeling that "the war will be won or lost on the beaches," he set about strengthening the fortifications. He was on leave on D-Day, June 6, 1944 (*see pp. 1275–1289*), when the Allies invaded Europe. Rommel dashed back to the front but was severely injured on July 17 when

his car was strafed by Allied aircraft. During his convalescence, a group of anti-Nazi officers made an unsuccessful attempt to assassinate Hitler on July 20, 1944. Rommel, who had become openly critical of Hitler's policies and knew about the plot, was given the choice of suicide or a trial as a traitor. He swallowed poison to save his family from retribution. The Nazi government announced that he had died of his injury and buried him with full military honors.

ROOSEVELT, Franklin Delano (*Continued from Volume 14*). In 1940, Roosevelt sought and was elected to an unprecedented third term as President. He won despite opposition to a third term within his own party from Vice-President John Nance Garner (1868–1967), who had been replaced on the Democratic ticket by Secretary of Agriculture Henry A. Wallace (1888–1965); Postmaster General James A. Farley (born 1888), who refused to manage F.D.R.'s campaign and resigned from the cabinet; and John L. Lewis (1880–1969) of the United Mine Workers, who tried to swing the labor vote against the President. Roosevelt defeated Republican candidate **Wendell L. Willkie** (*see*) by nearly 5,000,000 popular votes and a decisive electoral vote of 449 to 82. Although the 1940 campaign was waged largely on domestic issues—both candidates agreed on the necessity for defense preparations and opposed American involvement in war—Roosevelt's third term was to be occupied almost exclusively with World War II. The growing belligerence of **Adolf Hitler** in Germany and **Benito Mussolini** in Italy (*see both*), as well as the actions of the militarists controlling Japan, had gradually moved the United States from its position of official neutrality to undisguised efforts to strengthen America and aid friendly powers in Europe (*see pp. 1265–1272*). In late 1937, Roosevelt had made his famous "quarantine" speech, in which he advocated that free nations halt all trade with Japan and Germany. The President's appeal in 1939 to Hitler and Mussolini to abandon their aggressive policies went unheeded. The following year, despite bitter opposition from isolationists who branded him a warmonger, the President persuaded Congress to authorize the nation's first peacetime draft through the Selective Training and Service Act. Addressing Congress in January, 1941, Roosevelt, in his memorable "Four Freedoms" speech, asserted that all peoples of the world had the right to "four essential human freedoms"— freedom of speech and expression, freedom of worship, freedom from want, and freedom from fear. Two months later, Congress enacted the Lend-Lease program to aid the Allies and make the United States "the arsenal of democracy" (*see pp. 1269–1270*). In July, Japanese assets in America were frozen, and in August Roosevelt met with British Prime Minister **Winston Churchill** at sea off Newfoundland to draw up the **Atlantic Charter** (*see both*), a joint statement of international objectives. Roosevelt's last-minute appeal to Emperor Hirohito (born 1901) failed to prevent the Japanese attack on Pearl Harbor on December 7, 1941. The following day, the President requested and received from Congress a declaration of war on Japan. Within a week, America was also at war with Germany and Italy. Roosevelt quickly mobilized the nation. A military force was raised that included 15,000,000 men and women before the conflict

was over. Numerous federal agencies were created to secure maximum output from labor and industry, and wage and price controls were instituted to curb inflation (*see pp. 1336–1338*). Many able administrators were enlisted to run the giant wartime bureaucracy, but Roosevelt himself maintained a close rein and final authority on these civilian organizations. He also directed foreign policy, working out war strategy and postwar agreements with Churchill and Russian Premier **Joseph Stalin** during the **Teheran** and **Yalta Conferences** (*see all*) and establishing close liaison with other Allied leaders (*see* **Cairo** and **Casablanca Conferences**). In July, 1944, the President conferred at Pearl Harbor with General **Douglas MacArthur** and Admiral **Chester W. Nimitz** (*see both*) on Allied strategy in the Pacific Theater. While prosecuting the war, Roosevelt also strove to lay the foundations for postwar international cooperation in his meetings with Allied chiefs of state. The good-neighbor policy, begun during his first term as President, helped assure virtual "hemisphere solidarity," with all Latin-American nations, except Argentina, supporting the Allies. In 1944, Roosevelt, running on a ticket with **Harry S. Truman** (*see*), was returned to office for his fourth term by defeating Republican candidate **Thomas E. Dewey** (*see*) by 3,500,000 popular votes and 432 electoral votes to Dewey's 99. For nearly three and a half years, Roosevelt directed the course of the war as Allied forces relentlessly wore down the Axis aggressors (*see pp. 1275–1310*). The deterioration of his health was evident in February, 1945, when he attended the Yalta Conference (*see p. 1332*). On April 12, less than a month before the surrender of Germany,

Roosevelt, President of the United States for just over 12 years, died of a cerebral hemorrhage at the health resort of Warm Springs, Georgia. Vice-President Truman (*see p. 1338*) took the Presidential oath of office that evening. Roosevelt was buried on the family estate at Hyde Park, New York.

S

SMITH, Walter Bedell (1895–1961). A soldier, statesman, and diplomat, Smith served as Chief of Staff for General **Dwight D. Eisenhower** (*see*) during World War II and afterward had a major role in planning the nation's cold-war strategy. A native of Indianapolis, Smith joined the Indiana national guard at the age of 15. Transferring to the army in World War I, he was commissioned a lieutenant and saw action in France, where he was wounded. For 20 years following the war, Smith attended army training schools and served at military posts in the United States and the Philippines. At the time of the outbreak of World War II in Europe in 1939, Smith held the rank of major and was an assistant secretary to the War Department general staff. In 1942, Smith, now a brigadier general, was sent to London to become chief of staff for Eisenhower in the European Theater of Operations. Smith's services soon proved so indispensable that Eisenhower referred to him as his general manager and said he was the best chief of staff any commander ever had. Smith was instrumental in planning the Allied landings in North Africa in November, 1942, and the offensive through Sicily to the Italian mainland in the summer of 1943. He secretly negotiated the surrender of the Italian government in September of that same year. Later, at Supreme Headquarters, Allied Expeditionary Forces (SHAEF), he helped organize the massive invasion of France on D-Day, June 6, 1944 (*see pp. 1275–1289*). Acting for Eisenhower, Smith accepted the unconditional surrender of Nazi Germany at Reims, France, on May 7, 1945. Smith was subsequently promoted to lieutenant general and in 1951 to full general. Meanwhile, in 1946, President **Harry S. Truman** (*see*) had appointed him to the sensitive diplomatic post of ambassador to Russia. In Moscow, Smith conducted hard-line diplomacy with the Soviets, whose government he described as "nailed in place by bayonets and held together by an omnipresent demonstration of force." When the Communists invaded Korea in 1950, Smith was appointed director of the Central Intelligence Agency to revamp the nation's information-gathering operations throughout the world. Three years later, Eisenhower, now the President, named him Undersecretary of State. As such, Smith led the United States delegation at the Geneva Conference on Far Eastern Affairs in 1954, at which the question of Korean unification was discussed and an armistice was reached in Indochina between North Vietnam and France. Later that year, he resigned to join the American Machine and Foundry Company, though he continued to serve as a special adviser to the government.

SPRUANCE, Raymond Ames (1886–1969). Spruance relieved the ailing Admiral **William F. Halsey** (*see*) at Midway in June, 1942, and emerged the hero of that crucial battle (*see pp. 1294–1295*). Born in Baltimore, Spruance graduated from Annapolis in 1906. After further studies

in electrical engineering, he was electrical superintendent at the New York Navy Yard after the United States' entry into World War I. Following nearly 20 years of peacetime duty on land and at sea, Spruance was given command of the battleship *Mississippi* in 1938, and the following year he was promoted to rear admiral. Three months before the Japanese attack on Pearl Harbor on December 7, 1941, he took over command of a cruiser division in the Pacific. At the Battle of Midway, dive bombers from Spruance's carriers managed to sink four Japanese carriers, while only one American carrier was lost. The battle was the first decisive United States victory in the Pacific and ended Japanese hopes of destroying the American Pacific Fleet. Appointed to head the Central Pacific command in January, 1944, Spruance had charge of the invasion of the Marshall Islands and the attack on Truk. That April, he was given command of the United States Fifth Fleet and attacked Saipan, Guam, and Tinian in the Mariana Islands (*see p. 1299*). On June 19–20, 1944, during the Battle of the Philippine Sea—popularly known as the Marianas Turkey Shoot—carrier pilots under Spruance's second in command, Rear Admiral Marc A. Mitscher (1887–1947), destroyed almost 400 Japanese planes and with the help of submarines sank three carriers, including Japan's newest and largest, the *Taiho,* and damaged two others. American plane losses totaled only 29. In the spring of 1945, Spruance had overall tactical command of the invasion of Okinawa. That November, he succeeded Admiral **Chester W. Nimitz** (*see*) as commander in chief of the Pacific Fleet. Spruance retired from active duty in 1948. President

Harry S. Truman (*see*) appointed him ambassador to the Philippines in 1952. He served for three years until his retirement.

STALIN, Joseph Vissarionovich (1879–1953). A tough, cold-blooded dictator, Stalin ruled Russia with an iron hand for 24 years (1929–1953). During this time, he directed her conversion from a basically agricultural country to an industrial world power—and ruthlessly liquidated all who opposed him. Stalin was born in the village of Gori, Georgia, in the Caucasus, the son of an impoverished and hard-drinking shoemaker who beat him frequently. His family name was Dzhugashvili, but he adopted the name of Stalin— "man of steel"—about 1913. He studied (1894–1899) for the priesthood, but while in a Russian Orthodox seminary he became a convert to the socialist philosophy of Karl Marx (1818–1883), and his radical political activities led to his expulsion in 1899. Stalin became an underground agitator opposed to the czarist regime ruling Russia. After the revolutionary leader Nikolai Lenin (1870–1924) caused a split in the Russian Social-Democratic Workers' Party in 1903, Stalin took sides with Lenin and the militant Bolsheviks against the more moderate Mensheviks. In the years preceding the Russian Revolution of 1917, Stalin rose steadily to power in revolutionary circles. He organized strikes, led robberies to obtain money for the party, and helped to found and edit the Bolshevik propaganda organ, *Pravda*. Between 1902 and 1913, he was arrested and jailed on five occasions and several times exiled, but escaped repeatedly. He was imprisoned in Siberia from 1913 to 1917. After taking part in the successful October Revolution of 1917,

Stalin became a close associate of Lenin and was appointed general secretary of the Communist Party in 1922, a position he used to fill the party's bureaucracy with men loyal to him. A few months before his death in 1924, Lenin warned of Stalin's growing power, but he died before he could take action against him. After Lenin's death, Stalin formed an alliance of party leaders against his chief rival for power, Leon Trotsky (1877–1940), the commissar of war, who was expelled from party councils in 1926. Stalin then turned on his former allies and by 1929 had become sole dictator of Russia. Through a series of "purge" trials in Moscow between 1934 and 1939, Stalin executed all his former allies and thousands of their followers. The Red Army was also purged. Trotsky, who had left Russia in 1929, was assassinated in Mexico by an agent of Stalin's 11 years later. Temporarily abandoning plans for world revolution, Stalin concentrated on "socialism in one country." Sweeping programs to industrialize Russia and collectivize agriculture—"Five-Year Plans" —were begun in 1928. Millions of peasants who resisted the collectivization of their farms were murdered. Throughout Stalin's rule, arms production and heavy industry were emphasized to the neglect of housing and consumer goods. Art, science, and history became vehicles for propaganda. In 1939, after failing to get British and French support for Czechoslovakia (see **Neville Chamberlain**), Stalin joined **Adolf Hitler** (see) in attacking Poland and then invaded Finland. Hitler subsequently turned on him and attacked Russia in 1941. The Red Army, weakened by the purge of its officer corps in the 1930s, fell back to Moscow.

However, Stalin refused to leave the city and became a symbol of resistance to his people. Until 1941, when he became premier, Stalin's only official position was head of the Communist Party. In 1943, he took the title of field marshal and two years later named himself generalissimo. At the wartime Allied meetings (see **Potsdam, Teheran,** and **Yalta Conferences**), Stalin proved a determined and shrewd diplomat. After World War II, Stalin established Communist regimes in all the Eastern European states occupied by the Red Army and directed Russia in a massive arms race with the United States. He backed the North Korean invasion of South Korea in 1950. Stalin died of a brain hemorrhage at the age of 74. In 1961, his body was removed from its place of honor in the Lenin Mausoleum in Moscow's Red Square and reburied in a simple plot during a period of "de-Stalinization" instituted by Soviet Premier Nikita Khrushchev (1894–1971). His daughter by a second marriage, Svetlana Alliluyeva (born 1926), defected to the United States in 1967.

STETTINIUS, Edward Reilley, Jr. (1900–1949). As Secretary of State at the close of World War II, Stettinius worked to build a permanent peace through the United Nations (see pp. 1311–1331). The Chicago-born statesman left the University of Virginia in 1924 without receiving a degree and took a job as a stockroom clerk for 44¢ an hour. Two years later, he went to work for General Motors, and by 1931 he had risen to the position of vice-president in charge of industrial and public relations. He was hired by the United States Steel Corporation in 1934 and within four years had become chairman of the board. In 1939, President **Franklin D. Roosevelt**

(see), who was seeking talented people from big business to work for the government, appointed Stettinius chairman of the War Resources Board. The following year, Stettinius gave up his interests in private industry and devoted himself to public service. As director of priorities in the Office of Production Management in 1941, he advocated the development of synthetic rubber. Later, as Lend-Lease administrator, he successfully defended before Congress the program to aid Great Britain. After being appointed Undersecretary of State by Roosevelt in 1943, Stettinius participated in the Dumbarton Oaks Conference in Washington, D.C., in 1944, at which the charter for the United Nations was drawn up. In December, 1944, Stettinius succeeded **Cordell Hull** (see) as Secretary of State and accompanied Roosevelt to the **Yalta Conference** (see) in February, 1945. Stettinius resigned that June to head the United States delegation to the United Nations conference at San Francisco. He resigned from this post in 1946 because of policy differences with the current Secretary of State, **James F. Byrnes** (see), and served as rector at the University of Virginia until ill health forced him to retire the year before he died.

STILWELL, Joseph Warren (1883–1946). A famous American commander and hero of World War II, "Vinegar Joe" Stilwell was a stern but respected general who was in charge of all American forces in the China-Burma-India Theater of war (1942–1944). Born in Florida, Stilwell graduated from West Point in 1904. He subsequently served in the Philippines and taught modern languages at West Point before fighting in France during World War I, where he was

"Vinegar Joe" personally led the Allied retreat from Burma to India in 1942.

awarded a Distinguished Service Medal. During peacetime service in the next two decades, Stilwell studied Chinese and attended the Command and General Staff School at Fort Leavenworth, Kansas. He served in China in 1926 with the Fifteenth Infantry and then as Chief of Staff of the American forces there. Later, he returned to China as military attaché at Peking (1932–1939). In March, 1942, Stilwell, now a lieutenant general, became chief of staff for General **Chiang Kai-shek** (*see*) and was appointed commander of the Fifth and Sixth Chinese Armies in Burma. He also assumed command of all American forces in the China-Burma-India area. Stilwell immediately went to the Burmese front, where the British were also fighting. Outnumbered and insufficiently equipped, his forces were badly defeated by the Japanese. He led the remnants of his army, as well as nurses and civilians—about 400 British, American, and Chinese persons in all—on a famous 20-day retreat into India through 140 miles of malaria- and cholera-ridden jungle. "I claim we got a hell of a beating," he remarked later in

New Delhi. "We got run out of Burma, and it is humiliating as hell. I think we ought to find out what caused it, go back and retake it." While awaiting reinforcements and supplies, Stilwell directed the bombing of Japanese installations in China and trained Chinese forces for a successful counterattack in Burma. In early 1944, he returned to Northern Burma with Chinese troops to protect the new Ledo Road, which connected with the old, famed Burma Road leading into China. This time, his Chinese and American troops slowly drove back the Japanese. In August, 1944, the victorious Stilwell was made a full general, but he was relieved of his Far Eastern command that October because of conflicts with Chiang Kai-shek, whose methods he had called "stupid" and "gutless." In January, 1945, he was made commander of the United States Army Ground Forces, and the following June he was given command of the Tenth Army in Okinawa. In September, after the defeat of Japan and the deactivation of the Tenth Army, Stilwell returned to the United States. At the time of his death, he was commander of the

Sixth Army, with headquarters in San Francisco.

T

TEHERAN CONFERENCE. The Big Three of World War II, President **Franklin D. Roosevelt** of the United States, Prime Minister **Winston Churchill** of Great Britain, and Premier **Joseph Stalin** of Russia (*see all*), met together for the first time in Teheran, Iran, from November 28 to December 1, 1943. Britain and America had finally decided to open a second front, and the purpose of the conference was to coordinate the Russian attack on Germany with the opening of the second front in France. It was decided that the invasion of France would take place in May or June of 1944. A landing on the southern coast of France from Italy and a stepped-up Russian offensive on the Eastern front would support the invasion. Stalin agreed that Russia would enter the war against Japan once Germany had been destroyed. The eastern boundary of Poland was altered to give the Soviet Union Russian-populated territory controlled by Poland between 1921 and 1939. Poland was to be compensated by receiving additional territory from Germany. In addition, the independence of Iran, which had been occupied by Britain and Russia since 1941, was to be reestablished. All three leaders agreed to support Josip Broz Tito (1892–1980), then the most effective of the partisan fighters in Yugoslavia, to strengthen resistance to the Germans there. Finally, it was agreed that postwar Germany would be partitioned in some way. Roosevelt and Churchill met in Quebec in September, 1944, and drew up tentative occupation zones for postwar Germany, which were later approved by Stalin at the **Yalta Conference** (*see*). Roosevelt, who stayed at the Soviet Embassy during the Teheran Conference, was quite impressed with Stalin and commented in his report to the nation Christmas Eve, 1943, "I 'got along fine' with Marshal Stalin, and I believe we are going to get along very well with him and the Russian people—very well indeed."

TOJO, Hideki (1884–1948). Known as Razor Brain, Tojo was a general who became prime minister of Japan during World War II and was responsible for leading his nation into defeat. Belonging to a family long associated with the army, Tojo graduated from the Imperial

Hideki Tojo

Military Academy in 1905 and from the army staff college 10 years later. In 1919, he was sent to Berlin as a military attaché to the Japanese Embassy. By 1935, Tojo had risen to the rank of lieutenant general and was appointed commander of the military police of the Kwantung Army in Manchuria. Two years later, he became its chief of staff. Thereafter, he planned an attack on Russia, using Manchuria as the base for the attack. This led to a major border war

with the Soviet Union in 1938–1939 that convinced the Japanese army that expansion into Russian Siberia was impracticable. Meanwhile, in 1938, Tojo had been recalled to Tokyo to become vice-minister of war in the cabinet of Prince Fumimaro Konoye (1891–1945). A military clique headed by Tojo dominated the cabinet, and in October, 1941, Tojo succeeded Konoye as prime minister. Once in control, Tojo's cabinet decided on war, reasoning that "rather than await extinction it were better to face death by breaking through the encircling ring to find a way for existence." Tojo remained prime minister until the fall of Saipan in July, 1944. After the surrender of Japan on September 2, 1945, he was tried as a war criminal. Convicted, Tojo was hanged in Tokyo on December 22, 1948.

TRUMAN, Harry S. (1884–1972). On April 12, 1945, in the closing months of World War II, **Franklin D. Roosevelt** (*see*) died, and Harry S. Truman—until then a relatively obscure political figure from the Midwest—became the 33rd President of the United States. "I felt," Truman would say later, "like the moon, the stars, and all the planets had fallen on me." As the Chief Executive, however, he was to be a leading figure in the postwar cold-war era, architect of the so-called Truman Doctrine to block Russian aggression, and the President who would lead the nation into its second major conflict in a decade, the Korean War. Raised on a farm near Independence, Missouri, Truman could not afford college and was rejected at West Point because of poor eyesight. Until the outbreak of World War I, he worked as a railroad timekeeper and as a bank clerk and then helped to run his family's farm. The

national-guard unit that he had joined in 1905 was mobilized in August, 1917, and Truman served in France as an artillery officer. After his discharge as a captain in May, 1919, Truman and an army friend opened a haberdashery store in Kansas City, only to see it fail in the recession of 1921. He later paid off all its debts. Another army friend, who was the brother of Kansas City's political boss, Tom Pendergast (1870–1945), convinced Truman to run for county judge. He was elected in 1922 but was defeated for reelection two years later. Truman, meanwhile, attended law school in the evenings, and in 1926, with Tom Pendergast's aid, he was elected chief judge of the county (1926–1934). Despite his association with the corrupt Pendergast machine, Truman won a reputation for honesty. In 1934, he was elected to the United States Senate and voted consistently for New Deal measures, even though Pendergast was anti-Roosevelt. However, his association with Pendergast kept Truman from establishing a rapport with the administration. Roosevelt tried to persuade Truman not to run in 1940. This only served to convince the stubborn, peppery Truman to make a primary fight against Roosevelt's choice as candidate. He won a narrow victory in the primary and then was reelected easily. Truman then urged the Senate to establish a special committee to investigate the national defense program because he was shocked by the waste and inefficiency he had seen at munitions plants and army bases while campaigning in Missouri. With Truman as chairman, the committee investigated defense expenditures and contracts. By 1944, the so-called Truman Committee had saved the taxpayers $15,000,000,000 by ex-

Vice-President Truman entertained Lauren Bacall at a G. I. canteen in 1945.

posing corporations that were manufacturing poorly made war goods. Truman had also become one of the most respected men in the Senate, no longer scorned by the administration. At the Democratic National Convention that year, many party leaders were intent upon dumping Vice-President Henry A. Wallace (1888–1965) because of his radical and pro-Russian views. When Truman was told that Roosevelt would support his nomination, he replied, "Tell him to go to hell." Roosevelt, however, increased his pressure on Truman, who finally agreed to be nominated. He defeated Wallace on the second ballot. Although Truman and Roosevelt got along well personally during and after the successful election campaign (*see p. 1338*), Truman's official duties were limited to presiding over the Senate and attending ceremonial functions. He was not even aware

of the **Manhattan Project** (*see*) to develop the atomic bomb. After Roosevelt's death in 1945 and after becoming President himself, however, Truman quickly took charge of the nation's war effort and assumed responsibility for all decisions that he made. He had a plaque installed in his White House office that read, "The Buck Stops Here." After just two weeks in office, the United Nations conference opened in San Francisco. A dispute arose over the seating of Poland, which had not been allowed to hold free elections as agreed by the Russian government at the **Yalta Conference** (*see*). Truman gave both the Soviet ambassador, Andrei Gromyko (born 1909), and foreign minister, Vyacheslav Molotov (1890–1987), a tongue-lashing. A compromise was worked out, and the charter setting up the United Nations (*see pp. 1311–1331*) was signed

on June 26. The war in Europe had ended May 7, and in July Truman traveled to Potsdam, Germany, to meet with Soviet Premier **Joseph Stalin** and British Prime Minister **Winston Churchill,** who later was replaced by **Clement Attlee** (*see all*). Truman took a strong stand at the **Potsdam Conference** (*see*), insisting that Russia modify her demands for huge reparations from Germany (*see p. 1335*). While there, he was informed that the atomic bomb had been tested successfully. Truman told Churchill of the successful test but only casually mentioned to Stalin that the United States had a "new weapon of unusual destructive force." Together with Churchill and Generalissimo **Chiang Kai-shek** (*see*) of China, Truman issued a warning that "the alternative [to surrender] for Japan is complete and utter destruction." Truman was certain that using the bomb would prevent another year of fighting and save perhaps 1,000,000 Allied casualties. With his approval—a decision that would later prompt much controversy— the first atomic bomb was dropped on Hiroshima on August 6, 1945. The city was virtually wiped out as more than 40,000 people were killed instantly and 60,000 others injured, many of them fatally. When Japan did not immediately capitulate, a second bomb was dropped on Nagasaki three days later, killing 36,000 people and injuring 60,000. Japan then surrendered on August 14, Truman consistently defended his decision to use atomic weapons. "Let there be no mistake about it, I regarded the bomb as a military weapon and never had any doubt that it should be used." However, his decision and other critical ones still in the future led Truman to write in the preface to his memoirs, "To be President of the United States is to be lonely, very lonely at times of great decisions." This was borne out in the years ahead, as East and West—once allies—grew increasingly apart. (*Entry continues in Volume 16.*)

U

UREY, Harold Clayton (1893–1981). One of America's foremost physical chemists, Urey played a vital role in the development of the first atomic bomb and later became a leading spokesman for the control of nuclear weapons. A pioneer in the separation of isotopes by chemical methods, he received the 1934 Nobel Prize in chemistry for his discovery of deuterium, or heavy hydrogen. Urey was born in Indiana and received his PhD degree from the University of California at Berkeley in 1923. After postdoctoral study abroad, Urey taught chemistry at Montana, Johns Hopkins, and Columbia Universities. It was while at Columbia in 1931 that Urey, with the aid of two other scientists, discovered deuterium, a breakthrough that greatly assisted the ability to control nuclear fission. During World War II, Urey directed the development of a gas-diffusion method for the large-scale separation of the uranium-235 isotope. This was an important step in the development of the atomic bomb, then being carried forward in the **Manhattan Project** (*see*). After the war, Urey and other scientists warned that consideration should be given to the ethical problems raised by the manufacture of nuclear weapons. Urey returned to teaching chemistry at the University of Chicago, until he resigned in 1958, when he was named professor-at-large of chemistry at the University of California at La Jolla. He also became interested in cosmology and published *The Planets: Their Origin and Development* (1952), in which he investigated chemical aspects of problems involved in the origin and evolution of the solar system.

W

WADSWORTH, James Wolcott, Jr. (1877–1952). A Republican Congressman from New York, Wadsworth introduced the nation's first peacetime conscription bill. After graduating from Yale in 1898, Wadsworth served in the Spanish-American War. Afterward, he settled in his native New York State to farm and raise livestock. Wadsworth began his political career in 1905 as a member (1905–1910) of the state assembly. He served seven times as a delegate to the Republican National Convention. In 1914, Wadsworth was elected to the United States Senate. Although reelected in 1920, he was defeated in his bid for a third term in 1926. He returned to farming and six years later was elected to the first of nine terms (1933–1951) in the House of Representatives. In 1940, in a bipartisan gesture, Wadsworth introduced with Democratic Senator Edward R. Burke (1880–1968) the first peacetime draft bill to Congress. The bill was later passed as the Selective Training and Service Act. Wadsworth retired from the House in 1951. That same year, President **Harry S. Truman** (*see*) appointed him chairman of the National Security Training Commission, a position he held until his death.

WAINWRIGHT, Jonathan Mayhew (1883–1953). Although defeated by the Japanese at Bataan and Corregidor early in 1942, Wainwright, the American in command of all armed forces in the Philippines, was awarded the Medal of Honor for heroically resisting overwhelming Japanese armies. The son of a career army officer, Wainwright was born in Walla Walla, Washington. After graduation from West Point in 1906, he became a cavalry officer. He went to France during World War I as a staff officer of the Eighty-third Division. Following the war, he served at various army posts and by 1940 was a major general and second in command to General **Douglas MacArthur** (*see*) in the Philippines. After most of the Philip-

Urey was one of the scientists chosen in 1969 to examine the first moon rocks.

Wainwright was forced to broadcast the surrender of Corregidor.

pine air force was wiped out by the surprise Japanese attack on December 8, 1941 (it was December 7 at Pearl Harbor, which is east of the international date line), surrender seemed inevitable. However, all forces in the Philippines were directed to fight as long as possible to gain time for the United States to organize an offensive. By Christmas, MacArthur had abandoned Manila, the capital, and ordered a retreat to the jungles and swamps of Bataan Peninsula and, if necessary, to Corregidor, an island fortress. In March, 1942, MacArthur, under direct orders from President **Franklin D. Roosevelt** (*see*), left for Australia to organize the Allied Southwest Pacific Command, leaving Wainwright in command. On April 9, 78,000 of Bataan's starving and ill-equipped defenders surrendered. They were forced to march nearly 60 miles north to a prison camp in a trek that became known as the Death March because between 7,000 and 10,000 prisoners died along the way. Meanwhile, Wainwright and

about 13,000 American and Filipino troops, civilians, and nurses had retreated to Corregidor. The majority of them lived in a large tunnel under the central hill. They resisted for 26 more days. By May 4, Japanese 500-pound shells were falling at the rate of one every five seconds. The following night, Japanese troops landed on the island. On May 6, Wainwright surrendered all American and native troops in the Philippines to avoid the certain death of the units now trapped in the tunnel. Along with other senior officers, Wainright was sent to a prison camp in Manchuria, from which he was liberated by Soviet troops on August 24, 1945. He was aboard the U.S.S. *Missouri* when the Japanese surrender was signed on her deck on September 2.

WATSON, Thomas John (1874–1956). Watson was the founder of International Business Machines (IBM), which under his control (1914–1956) became a worldwide corporation whose products —especially its complex, giant computers—are used in the

world's most advanced industrial, scientific, and governmental operations. Watson, who was born in Campbell, New York, began his career at the age of 17 as a store clerk. From 1898 to 1913, he worked for the National Cash Register Company, where he rose to the position of general sales manager under the company's ruthless supersalesman, John H. Patterson (1844–1922). In 1914, Watson became president of the Computing-Tabulating-Recording Company, whose name he changed to International Business Machines in 1924. Watson obtained loans to finance expansion and instituted efficient sales and technical training programs for his staff. He developed a three-step sales technique—the approach, the demon-

Mr. and Mrs. Thomas J. Watson

stration, and the closing—based on the catchy idea that IBM sells service, not machines. He also plastered the firm's walls with such mottoes as THINK and insisted that his employees dress conservatively and that they sing ditties in praise of IBM from a company songbook. IBM became a pioneer in the production of electronic calculators and computers. In a break with its emphasis on large systems, IBM introduced a personal computer in 1981. In four years, the IBM PC captured 40% of the market.

WELLES, Sumner (1892–1961). A career diplomat who was an expert on Latin-American affairs, Welles served under President **Franklin D. Roosevelt** (*see*) as Assistant Secretary of State from 1933 to 1937 and as Undersecretary of State from 1937 to 1943. He was responsible for coining the expression "good-neighbor policy" to characterize the Roosevelt administration's objectives in South America. A native of New York City, Welles graduated from Harvard in 1914 and then, with the help of Roosevelt, an old family friend who at the time was Assistant Secretary of the Navy, found employment in the State Department. He held minor posts in Tokyo (1915–1917) and Buenos Aires (1917–1919) before becoming assistant chief (1920–1921) and then chief (1921–1922) of the Latin-American division of the State Department. During the 1920s, he performed various missions in Haiti, the Dominican Republic, and Honduras. Respected for his knowledge and clarity of thought, Welles, as Assistant Secretary of State, took the lead in reversing earlier United States policies of exploitation and dollar diplomacy in South American countries. In 1937, he was promoted to Undersecretary of State. Welles conducted a fact-finding tour of Europe for the President in 1940. The following year, he accompanied Roosevelt to the conference held on shipboard off the coast of Newfoundland with British Prime Minister **Winston Churchill** that produced the **Atlantic Charter** (*see both*). During World War II, Welles

Sumner Welles and F. D. R.

was instrumental in persuading most of the Latin-American countries to side with the Allies against the Axis powers. He also worked on plans for international cooperation that subsequently contributed to the founding of the United Nations (*see pp. 1311–1331*). By 1943, however, friction had developed between Welles and his chief, Secretary of State **Cordell Hull** (*see*), and Welles resigned to devote himself to writing on foreign affairs. His publications include *Naboth's Vineyard* (1928), *The World of the Four Freedoms* (1943), *The Time for Decision* (1944), *Where Are We Heading?* (1946), *We Need Not Fail* (1948), and *Seven Decisions That Shaped History* (1951).

WILLKIE, Wendell Lewis (1892–1944). A virtual unknown who entered national politics at the age of 48, Willkie rose to eminence by winning the Republican Presidential nomination in 1940. Later, during World War II, he attained stature as a statesman by preaching the doctrine of international cooperation as a means of achieving world peace. A native of Elwood, Indiana, Willkie received his bachelor's and law degrees from Indiana University in 1913 and 1916, respectively. He served in the army during World War I and afterward practiced law in Akron, Ohio. Moving to New York City in 1929, Willkie soon became a prominent lawyer on Wall Street and president of the Commonwealth and Southern Corporation, a utility holding company with operating units in 11 states. He first gained national prominence when he became the spokesman for private utilities in their struggle against the government-operated Tennessee Valley Authority, which sought to set up an extensive power-distributing system that would compete in many areas with the Commonwealth and Southern Corporation. Although he ultimately lost the battle, Willkie emerged as a critic of the economic policies of President **Franklin D. Roosevelt** (*see*). In 1938, Willkie, who was originally a Democrat, joined the Republican Party because of his opposition to many New Deal measures and because he believed the Democrats no longer fostered world peace or progress. With his big-business connections and fresh approach to politics, Willkie soon became an attractive candidate capable of filling the leadership vacuum that existed in the Republican Party in 1939 and 1940. Backed by business leaders within the party, a "Willkie for President" movement began, and during the Republican National Convention in June, 1940, he won the nomination on the sixth ballot. Although he waged a vigorous campaign, pledging greater unity among Americans, an end to unemployment, and a more prosperous America, Willkie received 22,300,000 votes to Roosevelt's 27,200,000 and carried only 10 of the 48 states. In defeat, Willkie, acting as a

Candidate Willkie arrived by stagecoach at a Wyoming political rally.

private citizen, fought isolationism and helped achieve national unity at a time of crisis by rallying the "loyal opposition" to support the President's foreign policies. He visited England at the height of the German air blitz in 1941 and the following year went, as Roosevelt's personal emissary, on a world tour that included Egypt, Russia, and China. In 1943, Willkie wrote *One World,* the title of which served as a campaign slogan when Willkie made a second bid for the Republican Presidential nomination in 1944. However, his belief that World War II would not be resolved by a military victory, but only by peace, and his insistence that Americans extend all possible aid to the Allies alienated many isolationist Republicans. After being soundly defeated in the Wisconsin primary, he withdrew from the race. Willkie then tried to incorporate his liberal views in the Republican Party platform but failed. He refused to endorse either the Republican Presidential candidate, Thomas E. Dewey (1902–1971), or Roosevelt. He died shortly before the national election in 1944.

Y

YALTA CONFERENCE. On the eve of an Allied victory in Europe, the most controversial conference of the war was held at Yalta, in the Russian Crimea, to discuss the final defeat of the Axis powers, the problems of occupation, and the creation of the United Nations. President **Franklin D. Roosevelt** of the United States, Prime Minister **Winston Churchill** of Great Britain, and Premier **Joseph Stalin** of Russia (*see all*), accompanied by their foreign ministers, met from February 4 through February 11, 1945 (*see p. 1332*). The American Joint Chiefs of Staff were convinced that Russia should enter the war against Japan to destroy Japanese military forces in Manchuria and China. Russia agreed to enter "two or three months after" Germany had surrendered. As the price for his intervention, Stalin demanded and received the southern half of Sakhalin Island, the Kurile Islands, and

control of the Manchurian railways and the naval bases at Dairen and Port Arthur on the Chinese mainland—all areas taken from Russia during the Russo-Japanese War (1904–1905). Stalin agreed to the postwar division of Germany that Roosevelt and Churchill had drawn up in a Quebec meeting in September, 1944. However, he said that any French zone would have to be carved from territory set aside for the Americans and the British. A committee was established to determine the sum of German reparations. The eastern boundary of Poland was set at the so-called Curzon Line, thus giving Russian-inhabited territory to the Soviet Union, while the western boundary remained unspecified. Russia agreed to expand the Communist government she had established in Poland to include non-Communist members and to hold "free and unfettered" elections as soon as possible. It had already been agreed by Churchill and Stalin at a meeting in Moscow in October, 1944, that Russia's sphere of influence would include Rumania, Hungary, and Bulgaria, while Britain would be dominant in Greece, and that the two nations would have equal influence in Yugoslavia. The Allied leaders at the Yalta Conference decided that a charter meeting of the United Nations (*see pp. 1311–1331*) would be held in San Francisco on April 25, 1945. Veto power was granted to the five major powers in the Security Council—China, France, and the Big Three. Stalin requested that all 16 Soviet republics be admitted to the General Assembly as individual members, and it was agreed that two, Byelorussia and the Ukraine, would be admitted individually. Roosevelt has been severely criticized for selling out to the Communists at Yalta and

The Allied leaders decided the shape of the postwar world at Yalta in 1945.

for naïvely assuming that they would live up to their agreements. However, at the time of the conference, the atomic bomb had not yet been perfected, and both Roosevelt and Churchill thought Russian aid was vital to end the war against Japan. Only a month after Yalta, Roosevelt expressed "bitter resentment" to Stalin over his failure to honor agreements concerning Poland.

YAMAMOTO, Isoroku (1884–1943). Commander in Chief of the combined Japanese fleet, Yamamoto was the architect of the surprise attack on Pearl Harbor on December 7, 1941 (*see frontend sheet*). A graduate of the Imperial Naval Academy (1904), Yamamoto had served in the Russo-Japanese War (1904–1905) as an ensign. In 1925, he was sent to Washington, D.C., as a naval attaché. There and later in London as a delegate to a naval conference in 1934, he became personally acquainted with many American naval officers, who found him highly intelligent and aggressive and a brilliant chess and poker player.

Yamamoto was promoted to vice admiral in the early 1930s and subsequently became vice-minister of the navy, chief of naval aviation, and Commander in Chief of the combined fleet. A gifted tactician and an advocate of combined air and sea warfare, Yamamoto began planning the daring air assault on the United States Pacific Fleet at Pearl Harbor in January, 1941. By November, the study was completed and became the basis for Combined Fleet Secret Operation Order No. 1, in which Yamamoto declared Japan's intention "to drive Britain and America from Greater East Asia." However, at the same time, he warned the Japanese army that the navy could guarantee control of the Pacific for no more than one year. The attack was a success—four American battleships were sunk and four others seriously damaged—but no American carriers were in the harbor at the time. In June, 1942, Yamamoto commanded the Japanese fleet in its attempt to capture Midway, a strategic island about 1,300 miles northwest of Honolulu.

Control of Midway would permit Japanese entry into Hawaiian waters and provide the Imperial Navy with the only base in the eastern Pacific. Instead, American Admiral **Raymond A. Spruance** (*see*), who had learned of Japanese plans when a coded message was deciphered, was able to sink four carriers while losing only one. In 1943, Yamamoto set off from Rabaul, New Britain, for an inspection tour of air bases in the upper Solomon Islands. Prior to his departure, his itinerary was radioed in a top-security code to officials in the war zone. The message was intercepted by American intelligence and decoded. With the knowledge of Yamamoto's schedule and an awareness of his insistence on punctuality, American pilots were able to intercept and shoot down his plane on April 18, 1943. The admiral's body was later found in the Bougainville jungle and returned to Tokyo for burial. His successor, Admiral Mineichi Koga (1885?–1944), said, "There was only one Yamamoto, and no one is able to replace him. His loss is an insupportable blow to us."

Isoroku Yamamoto